듣고 말하고 쓰는 영작문 패턴 연습

초등 영어 세 문장 쓰기

저자

Anne Kim

한양대에서 교육학을 전공하고 숙명여자대학교에서 TESOL 석사 학위를 받았습니다. 연령과 학습 시기에 맞는 효과적인 영어 교수법에 대한 연구를 지속적으로 진행 중이며, 그 연구 결과를 바탕으로 다양한 저서를 집필하고 강의 활동을 하고 있습니다.

대표 저서

〈초등 필수 영어표현 무작정 따라하기〉, 〈기적의 영어일기〉, 〈가장 쉬운 초등 영작문 하루 4문장 쓰기〉, 〈초등 영어 구동사 160〉, 〈초등 영어 한 문장 쓰기〉 등

듣고 말하고 쓰는 영작문 패턴 연습

초등 영어 세 문장 쓰기

저자 Anne Kim
초판 1쇄 인쇄 2024년 5월 3일
초판 1쇄 발행 2024년 5월 13일

발행인 박효상   편집장 김현   기획 · 편집 장경희, 이한경   디자인 임정현
교정 · 교열 진행 안현진   표지 · 내지 디자인 김민정   마케팅 이태호, 이전희   관리 김태옥
종이 월드페이퍼   인쇄 · 제본 예림인쇄 · 바인딩   녹음 YR미디어

출판등록 제10-1835호   발행처 사람in
주소 04034 서울시 마포구 양화로 11길 14-10(서교동) 3F
전화 02) 338-3555(代)   팩스 02) 338-3545   E-mail saramin@netsgo.com
Website www.saramin.com

책값은 뒤표지에 있습니다. 파본은 바꾸어 드립니다.

ISBN
979-11-7101-059-2 64740
978-11-7101-057-8 (set)

우아한 지적만보, 기민한 실사구시 사람in

어린이제품안전특별법에 의한 제품표시	
제조자명 사람in	전화번호 02-338-3555
제조국명 대한민국	주 소 서울시 마포구 양화로
사용연령 5세 이상 어린이 제품	11길 14-10 3층

듣고 말하고 쓰는 영작문 패턴 연습

초등 영어 세 문장 쓰기

Anne Kim 지음

사람in
saram
in.com

 **머리말**

다양한 글을 듣고 따라 쓰면서
영어 글쓰기를 익혀 봐요!

영어 글쓰기, 왜 배워야 할까요?

우리 어린이들에게 이제 영어 학습은 언어 습득을 넘어 문화와 사회를 이해하게 하는 중요한 수단입니다. 2022년 개정된 영어 교육과정에서는 '말하기, 쓰기, 제시하기'를 미래 세대가 반드시 익혀야 할 핵심 역량으로 강조하고 있습니다. 따라서, 주어진 상황과 목적에 맞게 자신의 감정이나 의견을 글로 표현하는 능력은 이제 선택이 아닌 필수입니다.

영어 글쓰기, 무엇부터 시작해야 할까요?

우리 주변에는 빌딩, 병원, 학교, 주택 등 다양한 건물들이 있습니다. 이런 건물들은 만들 때 사용하는 재료나 방식에 따라 모양이나 용도가 달라져요. 글쓰기도 이와 마찬가지입니다. 기본적인 문장 구조나 패턴을 알고 있다면 이를 기초로 다양한 형식과 내용의 글을 쓸 수 있죠. 이 책에서는 초등학생들이 쉽게 접근하고 학습할 수 있는 '그림 묘사하기', '내가 좋아하는 것에 대해 쓰기', '온라인 글쓰기', '순서를 나타내는 글쓰기' 등을 다양한 주제와 패턴으로 제시하여 영어 글쓰기의 기본을 다질 수 있도록 했습니다.

초등 영어 글쓰기를 쉽고 재미있게 학습하는 방법이 있을까요?

처음 글쓰기를 시작할 때, 모델 글을 통해 올바른 글쓰기 형식이나 패턴을 익히는 것이 중요합니다. 모델 글을 통해 문장 구조, 어휘 사용, 그리고 문법을 자연스럽게 익히게 되는 것이죠. 또한, 글쓰기와 함께 제시된 질문을 가이드 삼아 답을 적어 나가다 보면 어느새 글 한 편이 완성됩니다. 이렇게 모델 글을 따라 글을 쓰면서 글쓰기에 대한 자신감을 키울 수 있습니다.

매일 영어 글쓰기 연습을 시작해 보세요!

글쓰기는 생각을 정리하고, 자신의 감정과 의견을 다른 사람에게 전달하는 중요한 도구입니다. 영어로 글을 쓸 수 있으면 세계와 소통의 창을 열 수 있습니다. 이 책을 통해 영작문의 첫걸음을 시작하는 모든 학생들이 자신감을 가지고 영어 문장을 유창하게 작성할 수 있기를 바랍니다.

영작문 세계로의 여행을 시작할 준비가 되셨나요? 지금 바로 시작해 보세요!

Anne Kim

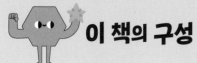

이 책의 구성

<초등 영어 세 문장 쓰기>는 다양한 주제에 맞는 글쓰기의 기본을 패턴 드릴을 이용해 연습할 수 있도록 듣기와 함께 단계별로 구성되어 있어요.

본문 구성 총 4개의 Step으로 구성되어 문장을 차례대로 연습합니다.

Read to Write

Unit에서 연습하게 될 세 문장으로 된 하나의 글을 모델로 보여 줍니다.

Step 0 패턴 이해하기

세 문장 각각의 패턴에 대한 정보를 주어 미리 인식하게 합니다.

Step 1 단어 파악하기

본격적인 패턴 문장 연습 전에 알아 두면 도움이 될 단어나 표현들을 듣고, 따라 말하고, 쓰면서 체화합니다.

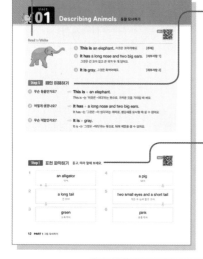

Step 2 패턴 문장 뼈대 잡기

Unit에서 익힐 패턴을 듣기와 함께 다양한 유형으로 연습합니다.
A 나열된 표현 덩어리(Chunk)를 연결해 써서 한 문장을 만듭니다.
B 듣고 빈칸을 채우며 패턴을 익힙니다.

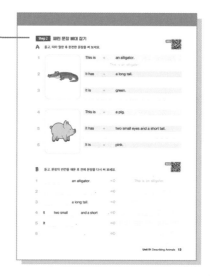

Step 3 패턴 문장 만들기

Unit에서 익힌 패턴을 듣기와 함께 복습하며 점검합니다.
A 주어진 단어나 표현을 알맞게 배열해 제대로 된 문장을 써 봅니다.
B 패턴을 제대로 이해했는지 한글을 보고 세 문장으로 된 하나의 글을 직접 써 봅니다.

Review Test

Unit을 몇 개씩 묶어서 비슷한 유형의 패턴을 한 번 더 복습합니다.

정답 및 해석

각 Unit과 Review Test 문제의 답과 해석을 제시합니다.

차례 및 학습 진도표

공부한 날 표시하기

Part 1	Unit 01 ____월____일	Unit 02 ____월____일	Unit 03 ____월____일	Unit 04 ____월____일	Unit 05 ____월____일	Review 01 ____월____일
	Unit 06 ____월____일	Unit 07 ____월____일	Unit 08 ____월____일	Unit 09 ____월____일	Review 02 ____월____일	
	Unit 10 ____월____일	Unit 11 ____월____일	Unit 12 ____월____일	Unit 13 ____월____일	Review 03 ____월____일	
Part 2	Unit 01 ____월____일	Unit 02 ____월____일	Unit 03 ____월____일	Unit 04 ____월____일	Unit 05 ____월____일	Review 04 ____월____일
	Unit 06 ____월____일	Unit 07 ____월____일	Unit 08 ____월____일	Unit 09 ____월____일	Review 05 ____월____일	
	Unit 10 ____월____일	Unit 11 ____월____일	Unit 12 ____월____일	Unit 13 ____월____일	Unit 14 ____월____일	Review 06 ____월____일
Part 3	Unit 01 ____월____일	Unit 02 ____월____일	Unit 03 ____월____일	Unit 04 ____월____일	Review 07 ____월____일	
	Unit 05 ____월____일	Unit 06 ____월____일	Unit 07 ____월____일	Unit 08 ____월____일	Review 08 ____월____일	
	Unit 09 ____월____일	Unit 10 ____월____일	Unit 11 ____월____일	Unit 12 ____월____일	Review 09 ____월____일	
Part 4	Unit 01 ____월____일	Unit 02 ____월____일	Unit 03 ____월____일	Unit 04 ____월____일	Review 10 ____월____일	
	Unit 05 ____월____일	Unit 06 ____월____일	Unit 07 ____월____일	Unit 08 ____월____일	Review 11 ____월____일	

영어 글쓰기 기초 다지기

다양한 형식의 글을 쉽고 재미있게 익혀요!

모델(Model) 글을 읽고 따라 쓰는 훈련은 영어 글쓰기를 익히는 효과적인 학습법입니다. 어떤 점들이 좋은 걸까요? 먼저 모델 글을 보고 올바른 문장 구조와 글쓰기 스타일을 익힐 수 있습니다. 또한, 모델 글에서 사용된 어휘를 활용하면서 새로운 단어들도 배울 수 있습니다. 그리고 글쓰기에 필수적인 올바른 문법을 자연스럽게 익히게 됩니다. 무엇보다도 모델 글을 따라 쓰면서 올바르게 글을 쓸 수 있다는 자신감을 키울 수 있습니다.

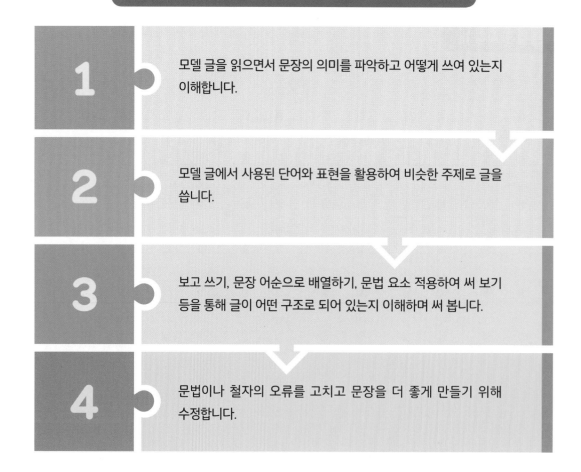

모델(Model) 글을 통한 영어 글쓰기의 효과적 학습법

1 모델 글을 읽으면서 문장의 의미를 파악하고 어떻게 쓰여 있는지 이해합니다.

2 모델 글에서 사용된 단어와 표현을 활용하여 비슷한 주제로 글을 씁니다.

3 보고 쓰기, 문장 어순으로 배열하기, 문법 요소 적용하여 써 보기 등을 통해 글이 어떤 구조로 되어 있는지 이해하며 써 봅니다.

4 문법이나 철자의 오류를 고치고 문장을 더 좋게 만들기 위해 수정합니다.

위와 같은 과정으로 글쓰기를 매일 꾸준히 연습하다 보면 모델 글을 기반으로 자신의 생각이나 경험을 더해 글을 완성할 수 있습니다. 처음에는 어렵게 느껴지겠지만, 점점 나의 생각을 표현하는 데 자신감이 붙을 거예요.

PART 1

그림 묘사하기

'그림 묘사하기'는 그림을 보고 그림 속 사물이나 상황을 생생히 설명하는 글쓰기입니다.

<그림을 묘사하는 방법>

1. 먼저 묘사하고 싶은 것이 무엇인지 생각해 봅니다.
2. 선택한 주제를 자세히 관찰하고 그림에 나타난 색깔, 크기, 특징 등의 키워드를 적어 봅니다.
3. 처음에는 간단한 문장을 사용하여 이해하기 쉽게 그림을 묘사합니다.

예를 들어, 사과를 묘사한다면 사과의 색깔, 모양, 맛에 대해 쓸 수 있습니다. 처음에 무엇을 써야 할지 잘 모르겠다고 해도 걱정 마세요. 주어진 질문을 보고 그에 대한 답을 글로 적어 나가면 도움이 될 거예요. 이렇게 질문을 가이드 삼아 답을 적어 나가다 보면 글을 쉽게 완성할 수 있습니다. 편하게 생각하고 글쓰기를 즐겨 보세요.

예시

주제	무슨 과일인가요?	**This is an apple.**
세부사항 1	어떻게 생겼나요?	**It is red and round.**
세부사항 2	어떤 맛이 나나요?	**It tastes sweet.**

Unit 01 Describing Animals 동물 묘사하기

Read to Write

1 **This is** an elephant. 이것은 코끼리예요. [주제]

2 **It has** a long nose and two big ears. [세부사항 1]
그것은 긴 코가 있고 큰 귀가 두 개 있어요.

3 **It is** gray. 그것은 회색이에요. [세부사항 2]

Step 0 패턴 이해하기

1 무슨 동물인가요? ⇒ **This is** + an elephant.
This is ~는 '이것은 ~이다'라는 뜻으로, 가까운 것을 가리킬 때 써요.

2 어떻게 생겼나요? ⇒ **It has** + a long nose and two big ears.
It has ~는 '그것은 ~이 있다'라는 의미로, 생김새를 묘사할 때 쓸 수 있어요.

3 무슨 색깔인가요? ⇒ **It is** + gray.
It is ~는 '그것은 ~이다'라는 뜻으로, 뒤에 색깔을 쓸 수 있어요.

Step 1 표현 파악하기   듣고, 따라 말해 보세요.

002

1
an alligator
악어
⇩

2
a long tail
긴 꼬리
⇩

3
green
초록색의

4
a pig
돼지
⇩

5
two small eyes and a short tail
작은 두 눈과 짧은 꼬리
⇩

6
pink
분홍색의

A 듣고, 따라 말한 후 완전한 문장을 써 보세요.

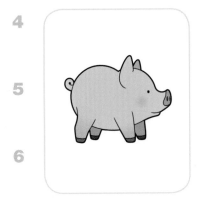

1   This is   +   an alligator.

This is an alligator.

2   It has   +   a long tail.

3   It is   +   green.

4   This is   +   a pig.

5   It has   +   two small eyes and a short tail.

6   It is   +   pink.

B 듣고, 문장의 빈칸을 채운 후 전체 문장을 다시 써 보세요.

1   _____ an alligator.   ⇨   *This is an alligator.*

2   _____ .   ⇨

3   _____ a long tail.   ⇨

4   It ____ two small ____ and a short ____ . ⇨

5   It _____ .   ⇨

6   _____ .   ⇨

A 주어진 말을 바르게 배열해 문장을 완성하세요. 듣고, 문장 확인 후 뜻을 써 보세요.

1 This / a giraffe / is   ⇨   This is a giraffe.

이것은 기린이에요.

2 has / a long neck and four legs / It ⇨

3 yellow and brown / It / is   ⇨

4 a penguin / is / This   ⇨

5 two short legs / has / It   ⇨

6 is / black and white / It   ⇨

New Words giraffe 기린 l neck 목 l leg 다리 l yellow 노란 l brown 갈색의 l penguin 펭귄 l black 검은 l white 흰

B 그림을 보고, 주어진 단어를 이용해 문장을 써 보세요.

이것은 앵무새예요.
그것은 깃털이 있어요.
그것은 노랗고 파래요.

parrot 앵무새   feather 깃털   blue 파란색의

CHECK!
CHECK!   ☐ 첫 글자는 대문자로 썼나요?   ☐ 구두점은 찍었나요?   ☐ 단어와 단어 사이는 띄어 썼나요?

006

Read to Write

① **Here is** a new alarm clock. 여기 새 알람 시계가 있어요. [주제]

② **It looks like** a robot. 그것은 로봇처럼 생겼어요. [세부사항 1]

③ **It has** two arms and two legs. [세부사항 2]
그것은 두 개의 팔과 두 개의 다리가 있어요.

Step 0 패턴 이해하기

① 어떤 물건인가요? ⇨ **Here is** + a new alarm clock.

Here is[are] ~는 '여기에 ~이 있다'라는 의미예요. 뒤에 단수(한 개)가 올 때는 Here is를,
복수(여러 개)가 올 때는 Here are를 써요.

② 무엇을 닮았나요? ⇨ **It looks like** + a robot.

It looks like ~는 '그것은 ~처럼 보인다'라는 의미예요. 여기서 like는 '~처럼'이란 뜻이에요.

③ 무엇이 있나요? ⇨ **It has** + two arms and two legs.

It has ~는 '그것은 ~이 있다'라는 의미예요. 사물이 가진 특성을 설명할 때 have 동사를 쓰
는데요, 여기서는 주어가 It이어서 has가 쓰였어요.

007

Step 1 표현 파악하기 듣고, 따라 말해 보세요.

1
a wizard hat
마법사 모자
⇩

4
a toy octopus
장난감 문어
⇩

2
a cone
원뿔, 고깔 모양
⇩

5
an alien
외계인
⇩

3
stars and a moon
별과 달

6
a head and tentacles
머리와 촉수

008

A 듣고, 따라 말한 후 완전한 문장을 써 보세요.

1	Here is	+	a wizard hat.
2	It looks like	+	a cone.
3	It has	+	stars and a moon.

4	Here is	+	a toy octopus.
5	It looks like	+	an alien.
6	It has	+	a head and eight tentacles.

009

B 듣고, 문장의 빈칸을 채운 후 전체 문장을 다시 써 보세요.

1 _____ a wizard hat. ⇨

2 Here _____ octopus. ⇨

3 _____ a cone. ⇨

4 It _____ an alien. ⇨

5 _____ stars and a moon. ⇨

6 It ____ a ____ and ____ tentacles. ⇨

A 주어진 말을 바르게 배열해 문장을 완성하세요. 듣고, 문장 확인 후 뜻을 써 보세요.

1 a cool kite / Here / is ⇨ _____

2 looks / It / like a bat ⇨ _____

3 has / It / two big wings ⇨ _____

4 is / Here / a new mouse ⇨ _____

5 It / like a ladybug / looks ⇨ _____

6 has / It / spots on its back ⇨ _____

(New Words) cool 멋진 I kite 연 I mouse (컴퓨터) 마우스 I ladybug 무당벌레 I spot 점 I back 등

B 그림을 보고, 주어진 단어를 이용해 문장을 써 보세요.

> 여기 가방이 있어요.
> 그것은 판다처럼 생겼어요.
> 그것은 큰 주머니가 있어요.

_____

_____

bag 가방   panda 판다   pocket 주머니

CHECK!
CHECK! ☐ 첫 글자는 대문자로 썼나요?   ☐ 구두점은 찍었나요?   ☐ 단어와 단어 사이는 띄어 썼나요?

011

Read to Write

1 **She is** my friend Sophia. 그녀는 제 친구 소피아예요. [주제]

2 **She has** long hair and blue eyes. [세부사항 1]
그녀는 머리가 길고 눈이 파란색이에요.

3 **She is** very friendly. 그녀는 아주 친절해요. [세부사항 2]

Step 0 패턴 이해하기

1 그 사람은 누구인가요? ⇒ **She is** + my friend Sophia.

She[He] is ~는 '그녀[그]는 ~이다'라는 의미예요. 뒤에 친구나 가족을 나타내는 말을 넣어 보세요.

2 어떻게 생겼나요? ⇒ **She has** + long hair and blue eyes.

She[He] has ~는 '그녀[그]는 ~이 있다'라는 의미로, 생김새를 묘사할 때 쓸 수 있어요.

3 어떤 사람인가요? ⇒ **She is** + very friendly.

She[He] is ~는 '그녀[그]는 ~하다'라는 의미로, 뒤에 사람의 성격을 나타내는 말이 올 수 있어요.

012

Step 1 표현 파악하기 듣고, 따라 말해 보세요.

1
Jack 잭
⇩

2
green eyes 초록색 눈
a round face 둥근 얼굴
⇩

3
funny 웃긴

4
Sandy 샌디
⇩

5
dimples 보조개
curly hair 곱슬머리
⇩

6
curious 호기심이 강한

A 듣고, 따라 말한 후 완전한 문장을 써 보세요.

1 He is + my friend Jack.

2 He has + green eyes and a round face.

3 He is + very funny.

4 She is + my friend Sandy.

5 She has + dimples and curly hair.

6 She is + very curious.

B 듣고, 문장의 빈칸을 채운 후 전체 문장을 다시 써 보세요.

1 _____ my friend Jack. ⇨

2 She _____ Sandy. ⇨

3 _____ green eyes and a round face. ⇨

4 She _____ and curly _____. ⇨

5 _____ very funny. ⇨

6 She _____ very _____. ⇨

015

A 주어진 말을 바르게 배열해 문장을 완성하세요. 듣고, 문장 확인 후 뜻을 써 보세요.

1 She / my friend Emma / is ⇨ _____

_____

2 has / long hair / She / and a round face ⇨ _____

_____

3 very friendly / She / is ⇨ _____

_____

4 my friend Tom / is / He ⇨ _____

_____

5 a big mouth / has / He / and dark hair ⇨ _____

_____

6 a little bit shy / is / He ⇨ _____

_____

New Words a little bit 조금 ǀ shy 수줍은

B 그림을 보고, 주어진 단어를 이용해 문장을 써 보세요.

그는 내 친구 조이(Joey)예요.
그는 머리가 짧고 눈이 파란색이에요.
그는 아주 용감해요.

_____

_____

_____

short hair 짧은 머리   brave 용감한

CHECK!
CHECK! ☐ 첫 글자는 대문자로 썼나요? ☐ 구두점은 찍었나요? ☐ 단어와 단어 사이는 띄어 썼나요?

Unit 04 Describing My Family 우리 가족 묘사하기

016

Read to Write

1. **She is** my sister. 그녀는 나의 언니예요. [주제]

2. **She is wearing** a uniform. [세부사항 1]
   그녀는 교복을 입고 있어요.

3. **She looks** amazing. 그녀는 멋져 보여요. [세부사항 2]

Step 0   패턴 이해하기

1. 가족 중 누구인가요? ⇨ **She is** + my sister.

   She[He] is ~는 '그녀[그]는 ~이다'라는 뜻이에요. 뒤에 가족을 나타내는 말을 넣어 보세요.

2. 무엇을 입고 있나요? ⇨ **She is wearing** + a uniform.

   She[He] is wearing ~은 '그녀[그]는 ~을 입고 있다'라는 의미예요. 현재 상황을 생생하게 묘사할 때 'be동사 + 동사원형-ing'를 쓰는데, be동사는 주어에 따라 am/are/is 중 골라 써요.

3. 어때 보이나요? ⇨ **She looks** + amazing.

   She[He] looks ~는 '그녀[그]는 ~해 보인다'라는 의미예요. look은 '~해 보이다'라는 뜻으로, 뒤에는 형용사를 쓰는 것에 주의하세요.

017

Step 1   표현 파악하기   듣고, 따라 말해 보세요.

1. my brother
   우리 오빠/형/남동생
   ⇩

2. blue jeans
   청바지
   ⇩

3. fantastic
   멋진

4. my grandmother
   우리 할머니
   ⇩

5. a dress
   드레스
   ⇩

6. lovely
   사랑스러운

A 듣고, 따라 말한 후 완전한 문장을 써 보세요.

1   He is   +   my brother.

2   He is wearing   +   blue jeans.

3   He looks   +   fantastic.

4   She is   +   my grandmother.

5   She is wearing   +   a dress.

6   She looks   +   lovely.

B 듣고, 문장의 빈칸을 채운 후 전체 문장을 다시 써 보세요.

1   _____ my brother.   ⇨

2   She _____ .   ⇨

3   _____ blue jeans.   ⇨

4   _____ a dress.   ⇨

5   _____ fantastic.   ⇨

6   _____ .   ⇨

A 주어진 말을 바르게 배열해 문장을 완성하세요. 듣고, 문장 확인 후 뜻을 써 보세요.

1 my mom / is / She ⇨

2 wearing / is / She / pants ⇨

3 She / young / looks ⇨

4 my uncle / He / is ⇨

5 is / wearing / He / a coat ⇨

6 He / great / looks ⇨

(New Words) pants 바지 I young 젊은 I coat 코트

B 그림을 보고, 주어진 단어를 이용해 문장을 써 보세요.

그는 나의 아빠예요.
그는 정장을 입고 있어요.
그는 멋져 보여요.

wear 입다   suit 정장   great 멋진

CHECK!
CHECK!   ☐ 첫 글자는 대문자로 썼나요?   ☐ 구두점은 찍었나요?   ☐ 단어와 단어 사이는 띄어 썼나요?

021

Read to Write

1 **They are** chefs. 그들은 요리사예요.　　　　　[주제]

2 **They work at** a restaurant. 그들은 식당에서 일해요.　[세부사항 1]

3 **They cook** delicious food.　　　　　　　　　[세부사항 2]
그들은 맛있는 음식을 요리해요.

Step 0 패턴 이해하기

1 그들은 누구인가요?　⇒ **They are** + chefs.

They[We] are ~는 '그들은[우리는] ~이다'라는 의미로, 뒤에 직업을 나타내는 말을 쓸 수 있어요.

2 어디에서 일하나요?　⇒ **They work at** + a restaurant.

They[We] work at ~은 '그들은[우리는] ~에서 일한다'라는 뜻으로, at 뒤에는 장소를 나타내는 말이 와요.

3 무슨 일을 하나요?　⇒ **They cook** + delicious food.

'They[We] + 동사(동작)'는 '그들은[우리는] ~한다'라는 뜻으로, 동사 뒤에 동사의 대상이 되는 말(목적어)이 올 수 있어요.

Step 1 표현 파악하기　듣고, 따라 말해 보세요.

022

1
zookeepers
사육사들
⇩

2
the zoo
동물원
⇩

3
take care of animals
동물들을 보살피다

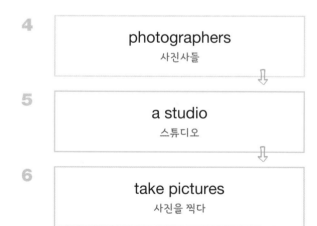

4
photographers
사진사들
⇩

5
a studio
스튜디오
⇩

6
take pictures
사진을 찍다

A 듣고, 따라 말한 후 완전한 문장을 써 보세요.

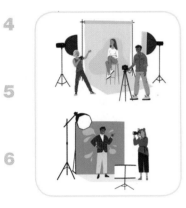

1	They are	+	zookeepers.
2	They work at	+	the zoo.
3	They take care of	+	animals.
4	We are	+	photographers.
5	We work at	+	a studio.
6	We take	+	pictures.

B 듣고, 문장의 빈칸을 채운 후 전체 문장을 다시 써 보세요.

1 _____ zookeepers.   ⇨

2 We _____ .   ⇨

3 _____ at the zoo.   ⇨

4 We _____ a studio.   ⇨

5 _____ animals. ⇨

6 _____ .   ⇨

Step 3 패턴 문장 만들기

A 주어진 말을 바르게 배열해 문장을 완성하세요. 듣고, 문장 확인 후 뜻을 써 보세요.

1 are / They / mechanics ⇨ _____

2 work at / They / the airport ⇨ _____

3 fix / They / airplanes ⇨ _____

4 police officers / are / We ⇨ _____

5 work at / the police station / We ⇨ _____

6 catch / We / thieves ⇨ _____

New Words) mechanic 정비사 | airport 공항 | fix 고치다 | airplane 비행기 | police officer 경찰관 | catch 잡다
thief 도둑(복수형은 thieves)

B 그림을 보고, 주어진 단어를 이용해 문장을 써 보세요.

우리는 우체부예요.
우리는 우체국에서 일해요.
우리는 사람들에게
편지를 배달해요.

_____

| mail carrier 우체부 | post office 우체국 | deliver 배달하다 |

CHECK!
CHECK!   ☐ 첫 글자는 대문자로 썼나요?   ☐ 구두점은 찍었나요?   ☐ 단어와 단어 사이는 띄어 썼나요?

A 우리말에 맞게 빈칸에 알맞은 단어를 골라 써 보세요.

1 이것은 코끼리예요. 회색이죠.

This is an _____. It is _____.

elephant / alligator   green / gray

2 여기 가방이 있어요. 그것은 큰 주머니가 있어요.

Here is a _____. It has a big _____.

bat / bag   pocket / wing

3 그들은 요리사들이에요. 그들은 식당에서 일해요.

They are _____. They work at a _____.

farmers / chefs   restaurant / studio

B 질문에 알맞은 답을 <보기>에서 골라 써 보세요.

1 What animal is it?   ⇨   This is a pig.

그것은 무슨 동물인가요?

2 What does it look like?   ⇨

그것은 어떻게 생겼나요?

3 What is she like?   ⇨

그녀는 어떤 사람인가요?

4 Who is he?   ⇨

그는 누구인가요?

5 What is she wearing?   ⇨

그녀는 무엇을 입고 있나요?

보기

It looks like a cone.   This is a pig.   He is my brother.

She is wearing pants.   She is very funny.

C 주어진 말을 바르게 배열해 완전한 문장을 써 보세요.

1 a long tail / has / It ⇨ It has a long tail.

2 pink / It / is ⇨

3 is / Here / a new mouse ⇨

4 is / wearing blue jeans / She ⇨

5 mail carriers / We / are ⇨

6 deliver letters / We / to people ⇨

D 문장을 보고, 틀린 부분을 알맞게 고쳐 문장을 다시 써 보세요.

1 we wOrk At the post office. ⇨ We work at the post office.

우리는 우체국에서 일해요.

2 they is Mechanics. ⇨

그들은 정비사들이에요.

3 he are My dad. ⇨

그는 나의 아빠예요.

4 sHe am wearing A coat. ⇨

그녀는 코트를 입고 있어요.

5 He Have short hair And blue eyes. ⇨

그는 머리가 짧고 눈이 파래요.

6 she are a little bit Shy. ⇨

그녀는 조금 수줍어하는 성격이에요.

026

Read to Write

1 **I play soccer after school.**
나는 방과 후에 축구를 해요.

[주제]

2 **I pass** the ball. 나는 공을 패스해요.

[세부사항 1]

3 **I also shoot** a goal. 나는 득점도 해요.

[세부사항 2]

Step 0   패턴 이해하기

1 방과 후에 무엇을 하나요? ⇨ **I** + play soccer + **after school.**

after school은 '방과 후에'라는 뜻으로 'I + 동사(동작) + after school'이라고 해서 방과 후에 하는 활동을 나타낼 수 있어요.

2 어떤 활동을 하나요? ⇨ **I pass** + the ball.

pass the ball는 '공을 패스하다'라는 의미예요.

3 또 어떤 활동을 하나요? ⇨ **I also shoot** + a goal.

shoot a goal은 '득점하다'라는 뜻이에요. also는 '~도'라는 의미로, 추가적인 내용을 덧붙여 말할 때 써요.

Step 1   표현 파악하기   듣고, 따라 말해 보세요.

027

1
play basketball
농구를 하다
⇩

2
throw the ball
공을 던지다
⇩

3
jump high
높이 뛰다

4
play the piano
피아노를 치다
⇩

5
read music
악보를 읽다
⇩

6
touch the keyboard
키보드를 치다

A 듣고, 따라 말한 후 완전한 문장을 써 보세요.

1		I play basketball	+	after school.
2	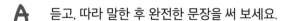	I throw	+	the ball.
3		I also jump	+	high.

4		I play the piano	+	after school.
5		I read	+	music.
6		I also touch	+	the keyboard.

B 듣고, 문장의 빈칸을 채운 후 전체 문장을 다시 써 보세요.

1 I _____ after school. ⇨

2 I _____ after school. ⇨

3 I _____ the ball. ⇨

4 _____ music. ⇨

5 _____ also _____ high. ⇨

6 I _____ the _____ . ⇨

패턴 문장 만들기

A 주어진 말을 바르게 배열해 문장을 완성하세요. 듣고, 문장 확인 후 뜻을 써 보세요.

1   I / yoga / after school / learn   ⇨ _____

_____

2   properly / I / breathe   ⇨ _____

_____

3   I also / on one leg / stand   ⇨ _____

_____

4   I / after school / dance   ⇨ _____

_____

5   shake / I / my body   ⇨ _____

_____

6   my arms / I also / stretch   ⇨ _____

_____

(New Words)   yoga 요가 I properly 올바르게 I breathe 숨을 쉬다 I stand 서다 I shake 흔들다 I stretch 뻗다

B 그림을 보고, 주어진 단어나 표현을 이용해 문장을 써 보세요.

나는 방과 후에 야구를 해요.
나는 공을 쳐요.
나는 공을 잡기도 해요.

_____

_____

_____

play baseball 야구를 하다   **hit** 치다   **catch** 잡다

CHECK! CHECK!   ☐ 첫 글자는 대문자로 썼나요?   ☐ 구두점은 찍었나요?   ☐ 단어와 단어 사이는 띄어 썼나요?

Unit 07 Describing Actions 2 행동 묘사하기 2

 031

Read to Write

1. **My mom is** in the garden. 우리 엄마는 정원에 있어요.[주제]

2. **She is** wate**ring** the flowers and plants. [세부사항 1]
그녀는 꽃과 나무에 물을 주고 있어요.

3. **She is** listen**ing** to birds sing, **too**. [세부사항 2]
그녀는 새들이 노래하는 것도 듣고 있어요.

Step 0 패턴 이해하기

1. 가족 구성원은 어디에 있나요? ⇨ **My mom is** + in the garden.

'주어 + am/are/is + in + 장소'는 '…가 ~에 있다'라는 뜻으로, 누가 어디에 있는지를 나타내요.

2. 무엇을 하고 있나요? ⇨ **She is** wate**ring** + the flowers and plants.

'주어 + am/are/is + 동사원형-ing'는 '…가 ~하고 있다, …가 ~하는 중이다'라는 뜻으로, 현재 하고 있는 동작을 나타내요.

3. 또 어떤 일을 하고 있나요? ⇨ **She is** listen**ing** to + birds sing, + **too**.

too가 '~도 (또한)'라는 의미로 쓰일 때는 문장 뒤에 와요.

 032

Step 1 표현 파악하기 듣고, 따라 말해 보세요.

1. in the kitchen
부엌에
⇩

2. cut some onions and mushrooms
양파와 버섯을 자르다
⇩

3. cook ramen
라면을 요리하다

4. in my room
내 방에
⇩

5. throw away the garbage
쓰레기를 버리다
⇩

6. sweep the floor
마루를 쓸다

A 듣고, 따라 말한 후 완전한 문장을 써 보세요.

1 My dad is   +   in the kitchen.

2 He is cutting   +   some onions and mushrooms.

3 He is cooking   +   ramen, too.

4 I am   +   in my room.

5 I am throwing away   +   the garbage.

6 I am sweeping   +   the floor, too.

B 듣고, 문장의 빈칸을 채운 후 전체 문장을 다시 써 보세요.

1 _____ in the kitchen. ⇨ _____

2 I _____ my _____ . ⇨ _____

3 He is _____ some onions and mushrooms. ⇨ _____

4 I _____ the garbage. ⇨ _____

5 _____ ramen, too. ⇨ _____

6 _____ the floor, too. ⇨ _____

Step 3 패턴 문장 만들기

A 주어진 말을 바르게 배열해 문장을 완성하세요. 듣고, 문장 확인 후 뜻을 써 보세요.

1 are / in the living room / My sisters ⇨

2 They / watching a movie / are ⇨

3 eating popcorn, / are / They / too ⇨

4 in her bedroom / is / My grandmother ⇨

5 She / listening to / is / music ⇨

6 is / too / writing / She / a letter, ⇨

(New Words) watch a movie 영화를 보다 ǀ listen to music 음악을 듣다 ǀ write a letter 편지를 쓰다

B 그림을 보고, 주어진 표현을 이용해 문장을 써 보세요.

우리 오빠는 욕실에 있어요.
그는 세수를 하고 있어요.
그는 이도 닦고 있어요.

wash one's face 세수하다   **brush one's teeth** 이를 닦다

CHECK!
CHECK!
☐ 첫 글자는 대문자로 썼나요?   ☐ 구두점은 찍었나요?   ☐ 단어와 단어 사이는 띄어 썼나요?

Describing My Town 우리 동네 묘사하기

 036

Read to Write

1 **I live in** a big city. 나는 큰 도시에 살아요. [주제]

2 **There are** a lot of tall buildings. [세부사항 1]
높은 건물들이 많이 있어요.

3 **There is** a long bridge. [세부사항 2]
긴 다리가 하나 있어요.

Step 0 패턴 이해하기

1 어디에 살고 있나요? ⇨ **I live in** + a big city.

I live in ~은 '나는 ~에 산다'라는 의미예요. in 뒤에는 나라나 도시 등의
장소가 올 수 있어요.

2 동네에 많이 있는 것은 무엇인가요? ⇨ **There are** + a lot of tall buildings.

There are ~는 '~이 있다'라는 의미로, 뒤에 복수 명사가 와요.

3 동네에 한 개만 있는 것은 무엇인가요? ⇨ **There is** + a long bridge.

There is ~는 '~이 있다'라는 의미로, 뒤에 단수 명사가 와요.

 037

Step 1 표현 파악하기 듣고, 따라 말해 보세요.

1
the countryside
시골 지역
⇩

2
a lot of trees and plants
많은 나무들과 식물들
⇩

3
a beautiful lake
아름다운 호수

4
a beautiful seaside town
아름다운 바닷가 마을
⇩

5
a lot of yachts
많은 요트들
⇩

6
a red lighthouse
빨간 등대

A 듣고, 따라 말한 후 완전한 문장을 써 보세요.

1		I live in	+	the countryside.
2		There are	+	a lot of trees and plants.
3		There is	+	a beautiful lake.

4		I live in	+	a beautiful seaside town.
5		There are	+	a lot of yachts.
6		There is	+	a red lighthouse.

B 듣고, 문장의 빈칸을 채운 후 전체 문장을 다시 써 보세요.

1 I _____ the countryside. ⇨

2 I live in a beautiful _____. ⇨

3 _____ a lot of trees and plants. ⇨

4 _____ a lot of _____. ⇨

5 _____ a beautiful lake. ⇨

6 _____ a red _____. ⇨

Step 3 패턴 문장 만들기

A 주어진 말을 바르게 배열해 문장을 완성하세요. 듣고, 문장 확인 후 뜻을 써 보세요.

1 in / live / a peaceful town / I ⇨

2 There / a lot of blue houses / are ⇨

3 is / a high mountain / There ⇨

4 in / I / a forest / live ⇨

5 are / a lot of huts / There ⇨

6 is / a tall waterfall / There ⇨

New Words peaceful 평화로운 I forest 숲 I hut 오두막 I waterfall 폭포

B 그림을 보고, 주어진 단어를 이용해 문장을 써 보세요.

나는 사막에 살아요.
낙타가 많이 있어요.
오아시스가 있어요.

desert 사막   camel 낙타   oasis 오아시스

CHECK!
CHECK! ☐ 첫 글자는 대문자로 썼나요? ☐ 구두점은 찍었나요? ☐ 단어와 단어 사이는 띄어 썼나요?

Read to Write

① **This is** the living room. 여기는 거실이에요. [주제]

② **My family usually talks** about our day. [세부사항 1]
우리 가족은 주로 우리의 하루에 대해서 이야기해요.

③ **We sometimes watch** movies **there**. [세부사항 2]
우리는 가끔 거기서 영화를 봐요.

Step 0 패턴 이해하기

① 집의 어느 장소인가요? ⇨ **This is** + the living room.
This is ~는 '이것은 ~이다'라는 의미로, 가까운 것을 소개할 때 써요.

② (거기에서) 무슨 일을 하나요? ⇨ **My family usually talks** + about our day.
family는 '가족'이라는 집합을 나타내는 말로 단수로 봐요. 이렇게 주어가 단수일 때는 일반동사 뒤에 -(e)s를 붙여요. usually는 '주로, 보통'이라는 뜻이에요.

③ 거기에서 가끔 어떤 일을 하나요? ⇨ **We sometimes watch** + movies + **there**.
sometimes는 '가끔'이라는 빈도를 나타내는 부사로, 일반동사 앞에 써요. always(항상), often(보통) 등의 빈도 부사도 같은 위치에 쓰면 돼요.

Step 1 표현 파악하기 듣고, 따라 말해 보세요.

1
my sister's bedroom
내 언니/누나/여동생의 침실
⇩

2
do one's homework every afternoon
매일 오후 숙제를 하다
⇩

3
play a board game
보드 게임을 하다

4
the kitchen
부엌
⇩

5
cook meals for my family
우리 가족들을 위해 요리를 하다
⇩

6
eat together
같이 먹다

A 듣고, 따라 말한 후 완전한 문장을 써 보세요.

1 This is _____ + my sister's bedroom.

2 She does her homework + every afternoon.

3 She and I sometimes play + a board game + there.

4 This is _____ + the kitchen.

5 My mom cooks + meals for my family.

6 We usually eat + together + there.

B 듣고, 문장의 빈칸을 채운 후 전체 문장을 다시 써 보세요.

1 _____ my sister's bedroom. ⇨

2 This _____ . ⇨

3 She _____ homework every afternoon. ⇨

4 My mom _____ for my family. ⇨

5 She and I sometimes _____ a board game _____ . ⇨

6 We usually _____ together _____ . ⇨

045

A 주어진 말을 바르게 배열해 문장을 완성하세요. 듣고, 문장 확인 후 뜻을 써 보세요.

1 This / our yard / is ⇨

2 reads / My dad / a book ⇨

3 there / dinner / My family / sometimes / has ⇨

4 the bathroom / is / This ⇨

5 washes / our hands and faces / My family ⇨

6 brush / I / there / my teeth / always ⇨

(New Words) yard 마당 l have dinner 저녁을 먹다 l wash one's hands and face 손과 얼굴을 씻다

B 그림을 보고, 주어진 단어와 표현을 이용해 문장을 써 보세요.

여기는 다락방이에요.
우리 엄마는 거기서 글을 쓰세요.
엄마와 나는 가끔 거기서
체스를 해요.

attic 다락방   play chess 체스를 하다

CHECK! CHECK! ☐ 첫 글자는 대문자로 썼나요?   ☐ 구두점은 찍었나요?   ☐ 단어와 단어 사이는 띄어 썼나요?

A 우리말에 맞게 빈칸에 알맞은 단어를 골라 써 보세요.

1 나는 방과 후에 축구를 해요. 나는 공을 패스해요.

I play _____ after school. I _____ the ball.

basketball / soccer   pass / catch

2 우리 아빠는 부엌에 있어요. 그는 라면을 요리하고 있어요.

My dad is in the _____. He is _____ ramen.

bedroom / kitchen   cooking / sweeping

3 나는 아름다운 바닷가 마을에 살아요. 빨간 등대가 있지요.

I live in a beautiful _____ town. There is a red _____.

country / seaside   yacht / lighthouse

B 질문에 알맞은 답을 <보기>에서 골라 써 보세요.

1 What do you do after school?   ⇨

당신은 방과 후에 무엇을 하나요?

2 Where is your mom?   ⇨

당신의 엄마는 어디에 있어요?

3 Where do you live?   ⇨

당신은 어디에 살아요?

4 What is this room?   ⇨

이 방은 무엇인가요?

5 What does your dad do in the   ⇨

kitchen? 당신의 아빠는 부엌에서 무엇을 하나요?

보기

My dad cooks meals for my family there.   My mom is in the garden.
I live in a big city.   I play the piano after school.   This is the living room.

C 주어진 말을 바르게 배열해 완전한 문장을 써 보세요.

1 is / This / my sister's bedroom ⇨

2 does her homework / She / every afternoon ⇨

3 are / a lot of yachts / There ⇨

4 live / in the desert / I ⇨

5 washing his face / He / is ⇨

6 also / touch / I / the keyboard ⇨

D 문장을 보고, <u>틀린</u> 부분을 알맞게 고쳐 보세요.

1 i jumps High. ⇨

나는 높이 뛰어요.

2 My Sisters is in the Living room. ⇨

나의 언니들은 거실에 있어요.

3 they am Watching a movie. ⇨

그들은 영화를 보고 있어요.

4 SHe are Writing a letter. ⇨

그녀는 편지를 쓰고 있어요.

5 there are a Long bridge. ⇨

긴 다리가 하나 있어요.

6 we Always eats together there. ⇨

우리는 항상 거기서 함께 식사해요.

Unit 10 Describing Food 음식 묘사하기

Read to Write

① **Look at** the chocolate cake. 초콜릿 케이크를 보세요. [주제]

② **It tastes** sweet and delicious. 그것은 달콤하고 맛있어요. [세부사항 1]

③ **It is** round and soft. 그것은 동그랗고 부드러워요. [세부사항 2]

Step 0 패턴 이해하기

① 무슨 음식인가요? ⇒ **Look at** + the chocolate cake.

Look at ~은 '~을 봐'라는 뜻으로, 이렇게 동사로 시작하는 문장을 명령문이라고 해요.

② 맛이 어떤가요? ⇒ **It tastes** + sweet and delicious.

It tastes[They taste] ~는 '그것[그것들]은 ~한 맛이 난다'라는 의미예요. taste 다음에는 맛을 나타내는 형용사가 와요.

③ 어떤 모양/촉감인가요? ⇒ **It is** + round and soft.

It is[They are] ~는 '그것[그것들]은 ~이다'라는 뜻으로, 뒤에 상태나 성질을 설명하는 말이 올 수 있어요.

Step 1 표현 파악하기 듣고, 따라 말해 보세요.

1
the lemon
레몬
⇩

2
sour and juicy
시고 즙이 많은
⇩

3
yellow and oval
노랗고 계란형인

4
the potato chips
감자칩
⇩

5
salty and crispy
짭짤하고 바삭한
⇩

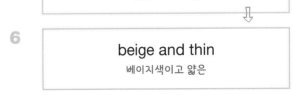

6
beige and thin
베이지색이고 얇은

A 듣고, 따라 말한 후 완전한 문장을 써 보세요.

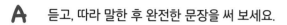

1		Look at	+	the lemon.
2		It tastes	+	sour and juicy.
3		It is	+	yellow and oval.

4		Look at	+	the potato chips.
5		They taste	+	salty and crispy.
6		They are	+	beige and thin.

B 듣고, 문장의 빈칸을 채운 후 전체 문장을 다시 써 보세요.

1 _____ the lemon. ⇨

2 Look ____ the _____ . ⇨

3 _____ sour and juicy. ⇨

4 They _____ and _____ . ⇨

5 _____ and oval. ⇨

6 _____ and _____ . ⇨

A 주어진 말을 바르게 배열해 문장을 완성하세요. 듣고, 문장 확인 후 뜻을 써 보세요.

1 at / Look / the pizza ⇨

---

2 It / salty and sweet / tastes ⇨

---

3 round and thin / It / is ⇨

---

4 at / Look / the ice cream ⇨

---

5 tastes / It / sweet and creamy ⇨

---

6 is / cold and soft / It ⇨

(New Words) creamy 크림 같은, 크림이 많이 든 ㅣ soft 부드러운

B 그림을 보고, 주어진 단어를 이용해 문장을 써 보세요.

치킨 너겟들을 보세요.
그것들은 바삭바삭하고 맛있어요.
그것들은 동그랗고 쫄깃쫄깃해요.

---

chicken nugget 치킨 너겟   **chewy** 쫄깃쫄깃한

 CHECK! CHECK! ☐ 첫 글자는 대문자로 썼나요?   ☐ 구두점은 찍었나요?   ☐ 단어와 단어 사이는 띄어 썼나요?

051

Read to Write

1 **I see** a pretty doll. 예쁜 인형이 보여요.　　　　　　[주제]

2 **It looks like** a princess. 그것은 공주님처럼 보여요.　　[세부사항 1]

3 **It is wearing** a pink dress. 분홍색 드레스를 입고 있네요. [세부사항 2]

Step 0 패턴 이해하기

1 무엇이 보이나요?　　⇨ **I see** + a pretty doll.

I see ~는 '나는 ~이 보인다'라는 의미예요. a pretty doll은 '예쁜 인형'이라는 뜻으로, pretty는 뒤에 나오는 명사 doll을 꾸며 줘요.

2 어떻게 보이나요?　　⇨ **It looks like** + a princess.

like는 '~처럼'이라는 뜻으로, It looks like ~는 '그것은 ~처럼 보인다'라는 의미예요.

3 무슨 옷을 입고 있나요?　⇨ **It is wearing** + a pink dress.

It is wearing ~은 '그것은 ~을 입고 있다'라는 뜻으로, 뒤에 옷이나 모자, 신발, 액세서리 등이 올 수 있어요.

052

Step 1 표현 파악하기 듣고, 따라 말해 보세요.

1	an action figure
	(영화 등에 나온) 영웅이나 캐릭터 인형
⇩	
2	a movie star
	영화배우
⇩	
3	a blue mask
	파란색 마스크

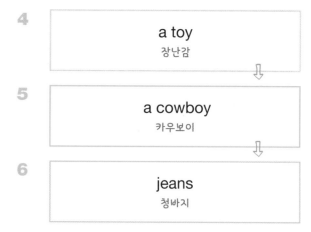

4	a toy
	장난감
⇩	
5	a cowboy
	카우보이
⇩	
6	jeans
	청바지

053

A 듣고, 따라 말한 후 완전한 문장을 써 보세요.

1 I see + an action figure.

2 It looks like + a movie star.

3 It is wearing + a blue mask.

4 I see + a toy.

5 It looks like + a cowboy.

6 It is wearing + jeans.

054

B 듣고, 문장의 빈칸을 채운 후 전체 문장을 다시 써 보세요.

1 _____ an action figure. ⇨

2 I _____ . ⇨

3 _____ a movie star. ⇨

4 It _____ a _____ . ⇨

5 _____ a blue mask. ⇨

6 _____ . ⇨

A 주어진 말을 바르게 배열해 문장을 완성하세요. 듣고, 문장 확인 후 뜻을 써 보세요.

055

1 see / I / a robot ⇨

2 It / a dog / looks like ⇨

3 wearing / It / sunglasses / is ⇨

4 see / a nice doll / I ⇨

5 looks like / It / an astronaut ⇨

6 wearing / a spacesuit / It / is ⇨

New Words sunglasses 선글라스 I astronaut 우주 비행사 I spacesuit 우주복

B 그림을 보고, 주어진 단어를 이용해 문장을 써 보세요.

(영화 등에 나온)
캐릭터 인형이 보여요.
그것은 슈퍼히어로처럼 보여요.
그것은 망토를 걸치고 있어요.

superhero 슈퍼히어로   cape 망토

CHECK!
CHECK!
☐ 첫 글자는 대문자로 썼나요?   ☐ 구두점은 찍었나요?   ☐ 단어와 단어 사이는 띄어 썼나요?

Unit 12 Describing People's Activities

사람들의 활동 묘사하기

056

Read to Write

❶ A woman and a baby **are on the grass.**   [주제]
한 여성과 한 아기가 잔디밭에 있어요.

❷ **They are playing** with a dog. 그들은 개와 놀고 있어요.   [세부사항 1]

❸ **The baby is singing** a song. 아기는 노래를 부르고 있어요.   [세부사항 2]

Step 0   패턴 이해하기

❶ 누가 어디에 있나요?   ⇨ A woman and a baby + **are on the grass.**

on은 '~ 위에'라는 뜻으로, be on the grass는 '잔디 위에 있다'라는 의미예요.

❷ 누가 무엇을 하고 있나요? (1) ⇨ **They are playing** + with a dog.

'They[We/You] + are + 동사원형-ing'는 '그들은[우리는/너는] ~하고 있다'라는 의미로, 지금 현재 하고 있는 동작을 생생하게 표현해요.

❸ 누가 무엇을 하고 있나요? (2)   ⇨ **The baby is singing** + a song.

'The baby[She/He/It] is + 동사원형-ing'는 '그 아기는[그녀는/그는/그것은] ~하고 있다'라는 의미로, 현재 하고 있는 동작을 표현해요. 주어가 단수일 때 be동사는 is를 쓰면 돼요.

057

Step 1   표현 파악하기   듣고, 따라 말해 보세요.

1
under the tree
나무 아래에
⇩

2
sit on a bench
벤치에 앉다
⇩

3
look at flowers
꽃을 보다

4
on the tennis court
테니스 코트에서
⇩

5
serve first
먼저 서브를 하다
⇩

6
hit the ball
공을 치다

058

A 듣고, 따라 말한 후 완전한 문장을 써 보세요.

1 A man and a woman are + under the tree.

2 They are sitting + on a bench.

3 They are looking at + flowers.

4 A man and a girl are + on the tennis court.

5 He is serving + first.

6 She is hitting + the ball.

059

B 듣고, 문장의 빈칸을 채운 후 전체 문장을 다시 써 보세요.

1 A man and a woman _____ the tree. ⇨

2 A man and a girl are on the _____. ⇨

3 They _____ on a bench. ⇨

4 He _____. ⇨

5 _____ flowers. ⇨

6 _____ the ball. ⇨

Step 3 패턴 문장 만들기

A 주어진 말을 바르게 배열해 문장을 완성하세요. 듣고, 문장 확인 후 뜻을 써 보세요.

1 is / A woman / in a dog park ⇨ _____

2 is / jogging / She / with a dog ⇨ _____

3 is / She / listening to music ⇨ _____

4 are / Two boys / in the woods ⇨ _____

5 are / They / birdwatching ⇨ _____

6 They / holding / binoculars / are ⇨ _____

(**New Words**) dog park 개 (전용) 공원 | woods 숲 | birdwatch 새를 관찰하다 | hold 잡다, 쥐다 | binoculars 쌍안경

B 그림을 보고, 주어진 단어와 표현을 이용해 문장을 써 보세요.

> 한 남자가 우리 앞에 있어요.
> 그는 사진들을 찍고 있어요.
> 그는 호랑이한테 먹이를
> 주고 있어요.

_____

_____

_____

in front of ~ 앞에   **cage** (짐승의) 우리   **take a picture** 사진을 찍다   **feed** 먹이를 주다

CHECK! CHECK! ☐ 첫 글자는 대문자로 썼나요?   ☐ 구두점은 찍었나요?   ☐ 단어와 단어 사이는 띄어 썼나요?

Describing Insects 곤충 묘사하기

061

Read to Write

1 **A butterfly is** on the leaf. 나비가 나뭇잎 위에 있어요. **[주제]**

2 **It has** two wings. 그것은 날개가 두 개예요. **[세부사항 1]**

3 **It is warming up** its body. **[세부사항 2]**
그것은 몸을 데우고 있어요.

Step 0 패턴 이해하기

1 무슨 곤충인가요? ⇨ **A butterfly is** + on the leaf.

on은 '~ 위에'라는 뜻으로, A butterfly is on ~은 '나비가 ~ 위에 있다'라는 의미예요.

2 어떻게 생겼나요? ⇨ **It has** + two wings.

It has ~는 '그것은 ~이 있다'라는 의미예요. have는 사람이나 동물, 곤충 등의 신체적 특징을 말할 때 쓸 수 있는데, 여기서는 주어가 It이어서 has를 썼어요.

3 무엇을 하고 있나요? ⇨ **It is warming up** + its body.

'It is + 동사원형-ing'는 '그것은 ~하고 있다'라는 의미로, 현재 하고 있는 동작을 생생하게 표현할 때 쓸 수 있어요.

Step 1 표현 파악하기 듣고, 따라 말해 보세요.

062

1
on the flower
꽃에

2
stripes
줄무늬

3
eat honey
꿀을 먹다

4
on the branch
나뭇가지에

5
shiny wings
반짝이는 날개

6
beat its wings
날개를 퍼덕이다

A 듣고, 따라 말한 후 완전한 문장을 써 보세요.

1
A bee is + on the flower.

2
It has + stripes.

3
It is eating + honey.

4
A dragonfly is + on the branch.

5
It has + shiny wings.

6
It is beating + its wings.

B 듣고, 문장의 빈칸을 채운 후 전체 문장을 다시 써 보세요.

1 A bee _____ the flower. ⇨

2 A dragonfly _____ the branch. ⇨

3 _____ stripes. ⇨

4 It _____ . ⇨

5 _____ honey. ⇨

6 _____ its wings. ⇨

065

A 주어진 말을 바르게 배열해 문장을 완성하세요. 듣고, 문장 확인 후 뜻을 써 보세요.

1   is / A grasshopper / on the rock   ➡

2   has / It / long antennae   ➡

3   It / leaping / great distances / is   ➡

4   is / on the ground / An ant   ➡

5   It / six legs / has   ➡

6   is / It / carrying / heavy loads   ➡

(New Words) grasshopper 메뚜기 I antenna 더듬이(복수형은 antennae) I leap 뛰다 I distance 거리 I load 짐

B 그림을 보고, 주어진 단어를 이용해 문장을 써 보세요.

무당벌레가 나뭇가지 위에 있어요.
그것은 검은 점들이 있어요.
그것은 느리게 기어가고 있어요.

ladybug 무당벌레   **branch** 나뭇가지   **spot** 점   **crawl** 기어가다

CHECK!
CHECK!   ☐ 첫 글자는 대문자로 썼나요?   ☐ 구두점은 찍었나요?   ☐ 단어와 단어 사이는 띄어 썼나요?

A 우리말에 맞게 빈칸에 알맞은 단어를 골라 써 보세요.

1 그 인형은 공주님처럼 보여요. 그것은 분홍색 드레스를 입고 있어요.

The doll looks like a _____. It is wearing a pink _____.

king / princess   hood / dress

2 한 여자와 한 아기가 개와 놀고 있어요. 아기는 노래를 부르고 있어요.

A woman and a baby are _____ with a dog. The baby is _____ a song.

sitting / playing   singing / sleeping

3 그 나비는 날개가 두 개예요. 그것은 몸을 데우고 있어요.

The butterfly has two _____. It is _____ up its body.

legs / wings   warming / crawling

B 질문에 알맞은 답을 <보기>에서 골라 써 보세요.

1 What does it taste like?   ⇨

그것은 어떤 맛인가요?

2 What do you see?   ⇨

당신은 무엇이 보이나요?

3 Where are they?   ⇨

그들은 어디에 있나요?

4 Where is the butterfly?   ⇨

나비는 어디에 있나요?

5 What does it look like?   ⇨

그것은 어떻게 생겼나요?

보기

It is round.   I see a pretty doll.   It tastes sweet.

A woman and a baby are on the grass.   It is on the leaf.

C 주어진 말을 바르게 배열해 완전한 문장을 써 보세요.

1 is / on the ground / An ant ⇨

2 black spots / has / It ⇨

3 on a court / are / A man and a girl ⇨

4 are sitting / They / on a bench ⇨

5 see / an action figure / I ⇨

6 a cape / is wearing / It ⇨

D 문장을 보고, <u>틀린</u> 부분을 알맞게 고쳐 보세요.

1 look At The pizza. ⇨

피자를 보세요.

2 They tastes Cold and Soft. ⇨

그것은 차갑고 부드러워요.

3 it look like A movie Star. ⇨

그것은 영화배우처럼 보여요.

4 we is holding Binocular. ⇨

그들은 쌍안경을 들고 있어요.

5 It Have six Leg. ⇨

그것은 다리가 여섯 개예요.

6 he is listens To music. ⇨

그녀는 음악을 듣고 있어요.

내가 좋아하는 것에 대해 쓰기

자신이 좋아하는 활동, 동물, 음식 등에 대해 자신의 생각이나 의견을 표현하는 글쓰기입니다.

<내가 좋아하는 것에 대해 글 쓰는 방법>

1. 먼저 내가 좋아하는 무엇에 대해 쓸지 생각해 봅니다.
2. 선택한 주제에 대해 어떤 점이 좋은지, 왜 좋아하는지 자신만의 이유를 생각해 봅니다.
3. 처음에는 어려운 단어나 문장은 피하고 이해하기 쉽게 설명해야 합니다.

예를 들어, 내가 좋아하는 반려동물에 대해 쓴다면 왜 좋아하는지 성격이나 특징 등 구체적인 이유를 적어 봅니다. 하지만 처음에 무엇을 써야 할지 모르겠다고 해도 걱정하지 마세요. 질문을 보고 그에 대한 답을 글로 적어 나가면 도움이 될 거예요. 이렇게 질문을 가이드 삼아 답을 적어 나가다 보면 어느새 내가 좋아하는 반려동물에 대한 글이 완성됩니다.

예시

주제	어떤 반려동물을 좋아하나요?	I like dogs.
세부사항 1	좋은 점은 무엇인가요?	They are always energetic.
세부사항 2	어떤 성격인가요?	They are cute and friendly.

066

Read to Write

① **My favorite friend is** Ben. 내가 가장 좋아하는 친구는 벤이에요.　　[주제]

② **He is** friendly to everyone. 그는 모두에게 친절해요.　　[세부사항 1]

③ **We both like** to ride a bike. 우린 둘 다 자전거 타는 것을 좋아해요. [세부사항 2]

Step 0 패턴 이해하기

① 친구의 이름은 무엇인가요?　⇨ **My favorite friend is** + Ben.

favorite은 '가장 좋아하는'이란 뜻으로, My favorite friend 하면 '내가 가장 좋아하는 친구'라는 의미예요.

② 어떤 친구인가요?　⇨ **He is** + friendly to everyone.

He[She] is ~는 '그[그녀]는 ~해요'라는 의미로, 성격을 나타내는 말이 뒤에 올 수 있어요. to everyone은 '누구에게나'라는 의미예요.

③ 친구와 공통점은 무엇인가요?　⇨ **We both like** + to ride a bike.

both는 '둘 다'라는 뜻으로 'We both like to + 동사원형'은 '우리는 둘 다 ~하는 것을 좋아한다'라는 의미예요.

067

Step 1 표현 파악하기　듣고, 따라 말해 보세요.

1
| Sally |
| 샐리 |
⇩

2
| quiet |
| 조용한 |
⇩

3
| read books |
| 책을 읽다 |

4
| Tom |
| 톰 |
⇩

5
| funny |
| 웃긴 |
⇩

6
| watch movies |
| 영화를 보다 |

068

A 듣고, 따라 말한 후 완전한 문장을 써 보세요.

1
My favorite friend is + Sally.

2
She is + very quiet.

3
We both like + to read books.

4
My favorite friend is + Tom.

5
He is + very funny.

6
We both like + to watch movies.

069

B 듣고, 문장의 빈칸을 채운 후 전체 문장을 다시 써 보세요.

1 My _____ is Sally. ⇨ _____

2 My _____ Tom. ⇨ _____

3 _____ very quiet. ⇨ _____

4 He ____ very _____ . ⇨ _____

5 ____ both ____ read books. ⇨ _____

6 We both _____ movies. ⇨ _____

Step 3   패턴 문장 만들기

A 주어진 말을 바르게 배열해 문장을 완성하세요. 듣고, 문장 확인 후 뜻을 써 보세요.

070

1 friend / is / Noah / My favorite ⇨

_____

2 is / very talkative / He ⇨

_____

3 We both / make jokes / like to ⇨

_____

4 friend / is / Emma / My favorite ⇨

_____

5 She / very curious / is ⇨

_____

6 like to / We both / play board games ⇨

_____

(New Words) talkative 수다스러운 ㅣ make jokes 농담하다 ㅣ curious 호기심이 많은 ㅣ play a board game 보드게임을 하다

B 그림을 보고, 주어진 단어와 표현을 이용해 문장을 써 보세요.

> 내가 가장 좋아하는 친구는
> 리암(Liam)이에요.
> 그는 아주 똑똑해요.
> 우리는 둘 다 컴퓨터 게임 하는 것을
> 좋아해요.

_____

_____

smart 똑똑한   **play a computer game** 컴퓨터 게임을 하다

CHECK!
CHECK!   ☐ 첫 글자는 대문자로 썼나요?   ☐ 구두점은 찍었나요?   ☐ 단어와 단어 사이는 띄어 썼나요?

071

Read to Write

1 **I really like** cake. 나는 케이크를 아주 좋아해요. [주제]

2 **It is** super sweet. Yummy! [세부사항 1]
그것은 아주 달아요. 아주 맛있어요!

3 **There are** many flavors. 여러 가지 맛이 있어요. [세부사항 2]

Step 0 패턴 이해하기

1 어떤 간식을 좋아하나요? ⇨ **I really like** + cake.

I really like ~는 '나는 ~을 아주 좋아한다'라는 의미예요. really는 '정말, 아주'라는 뜻으로 like의 뜻을 강조해 줘요.

2 어떤 맛인가요? ⇨ **It is** + super sweet. Yummy!

It is[They are] ~는 '그것[그것들]은 ~이다'라는 의미로, 뒤에 맛을 나타내는 말을 쓸 수 있어요. 가리키는 것이 단수일 때는 It is, 복수일 때는 They are를 써요.

3 어떤 특징이 있나요? ⇨ **There are** + many flavors.

There are[is] ~는 '~가 있다'라는 뜻으로, 여기서는 be동사 뒤에 복수 명사가 와서 There are가 쓰였어요.

072

Step 1 표현 파악하기 듣고, 따라 말해 보세요.

1
| gummy worms |
| 지렁이 모양의 젤리 |
⇩

2
| soft / tender |
| 부드러운 / 말랑말랑한 |
⇩

3
| different shapes and sizes |
| 다양한 모양과 크기 |

4
| potato chips |
| 감자칩 |
⇩

5
| crispy |
| 바삭바삭한 |
⇩

6
| many flavors |
| 여러가지 맛 |

A 듣고, 따라 말한 후 완전한 문장을 써 보세요.

1 I really like + gummy worms.

2 They are + soft and tender. Yummy!

3 There are + different shapes and sizes.

4 I really like + potato chips.

5 They are + crispy. Yummy!

6 There are + many flavors.

B 듣고, 문장의 빈칸을 채운 후 전체 문장을 다시 써 보세요.

1 _____ gummy worms. ⇨

2 I really _____ . ⇨

3 They are _____ and _____ . Yummy! ⇨

4 They _____ . _____ ! ⇨

5 _____ different shapes and sizes. ⇨

6 _____ flavors. ⇨

A 주어진 말을 바르게 배열해 문장을 완성하세요. 듣고, 문장 확인 후 뜻을 써 보세요.

1 like / I / dumplings / really ⇨

2 are / They / juicy / Yummy! ⇨

3 are / There / a lot of / ingredients ⇨

4 really / like / I / pizza ⇨

5 is / delicious / It / Yummy! ⇨

6 are / There / flavors / many ⇨

(New Words) dumpling 만두 I juicy 즙이 많은 I ingredient 재료

B 그림을 보고, 주어진 단어를 이용해 문장을 써 보세요.

나는 베이글을 아주 좋아해요.
그것들은 쫄깃쫄깃해요.
아주 맛있어요!
크림 치즈가 많이 (들어) 있어요.

bagel 베이글   **chewy** 쫄깃쫄깃한   **cream cheese** 크림 치즈

CHECK! CHECK!   ☐ 첫 글자는 대문자로 썼나요?   ☐ 구두점은 찍었나요?   ☐ 단어와 단어 사이는 띄어 썼나요?

Unit 03 My Favorite Superhero
내가 가장 좋아하는 슈퍼히어로

Read to Write

1 **My favorite superhero is** Spiderman.　[주제]
내가 가장 좋아하는 슈퍼히어로는 스파이더맨이에요.

2 **He is** brave and kind. 그는 용감하고 친절해요.　[세부사항 1]

3 **He can climb** walls and buildings.　[세부사항 2]
그는 벽과 빌딩을 탈 수 있어요.

Step 0 패턴 이해하기

1 좋아하는 슈퍼히어로는
누구인가요?
➡ **My favorite superhero is** + Spiderman.
My favorite superhero is ~는 '내가 가장 좋아하는 슈퍼히어로는 ~이다'란 뜻이에요.

2 어떤 성격인가요?
➡ **He is** + brave and kind.
He[She] is ~는 '그[그녀]는 ~하다'란 뜻으로, 뒤에 성격을 나타내는 말이 올 수 있어요.

3 무엇을 할 수 있나요?
➡ **He can climb** + walls and buildings.
can은 가능을 나타내는 조동사로, 'He[She] can + 동사원형'은 '그[그녀]는 ~할 수 있다'라는 의미예요.

Step 1 표현 파악하기 듣고, 따라 말해 보세요.

1
Flash
플래시
⬇

2
funny / fast
웃기는 / 빠른
⬇

3
run faster than lightning
번개보다 더 빨리 달리다

4
the Hulk
헐크
⬇

5
big / strong
큰 / 강한
⬇

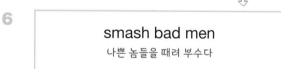

6
smash bad men
나쁜 놈들을 때려 부수다

A 듣고, 따라 말한 후 완전한 문장을 써 보세요.

1   My favorite superhero is   +   Flash.

2   He is   +   funny and fast.

3   He can run   +   faster than lightning.

4   My favorite superhero is   +   the Hulk.

5   He is   +   big and strong.

6   He can smash   +   bad men.

B 듣고, 문장의 빈칸을 채운 후 전체 문장을 다시 써 보세요.

1   _____ superhero is Flash.   ⇨

2   My favorite _____ the Hulk.   ⇨

3   _____ funny and fast.   ⇨

4   He _____ and _____ .   ⇨

5   _____ faster than lightning.   ⇨

6   He can _____ .   ⇨

A 주어진 말을 바르게 배열해 문장을 완성하세요. 듣고, 문장 확인 후 뜻을 써 보세요.

1 is / My favorite superhero / Aquaman ⇨

....

2 and cool / is / He / strong ⇨

....

3 can / He / breathe / underwater ⇨

....

4 is / My favorite superhero / Supergirl ⇨

....

5 is / She / kind-hearted ⇨

....

6 fly / can / She / in the sky ⇨

....

New Words   underwater 물속에서 | kind-hearted 인정 많은

B 그림을 보고, 주어진 단어를 이용해 문장을 써 보세요.

> 내가 가장 좋아하는 슈퍼히어로는 아이언맨이에요. 그는 매우 똑똑하고 놀라워요. 그는 문제들을 해결해서 다른 사람들을 도울 수 있어요.

....

....

....

Ironman 아이언맨   amazing 놀라운   solve a problem 문제를 해결하다

CHECK! CHECK!   ☐ 첫 글자는 대문자로 썼나요?   ☐ 구두점은 찍었나요?   ☐ 단어와 단어 사이는 띄어 썼나요?

Unit 04 My Favorite Subject 내가 가장 좋아하는 과목

Read to Write

① **P.E. is** my favorite subject. [주제]
체육은 내가 가장 좋아하는 과목이에요.

② **I am** really energetic. 나는 정말 활동적이에요. [세부사항 1]

③ **I like to** play soccer. 나는 축구하는 걸 좋아해요. [세부사항 2]

Step 0 패턴 이해하기

① 가장 좋아하는 과목은
무엇인가요?

⇒ **P.E. is** + my favorite subject.

'과목명 + is my favorite subject'라고 하면 '~은 내가 가장 좋아하는 과목이다'
라는 의미예요.

② 당신의 성격은 어떤가요?

⇒ **I am** + really energetic.

really는 '정말'이라는 뜻으로, really energetic은 '정말 활동적인'이라는 의미예
요. be동사 am 다음에 성격을 나타내는 말이 올 수 있어요.

③ 뭘 하는 걸 좋아하나요?

⇒ **I like to** + play soccer.

'I like to + 동사원형'은 '나는 ~하는 것을 좋아한다'라는 의미예요. like 다음에 동
사가 목적어로 올 때는 'to + 동사원형'의 형태로 쓰면 돼요.

Step 1 표현 파악하기 듣고, 따라 말해 보세요.

1
| social studies |
| 사회 |
⇓

2
| really curious |
| 아주 호기심이 많은 |
⇓

3
| learn about cultures and societies |
| 문화와 사회를 배우다 |

4
| music |
| 음악 |
⇓

5
| really joyful |
| 아주 즐거운 |
⇓

6
| play the piano |
| 피아노를 치다 |

A 듣고, 따라 말한 후 완전한 문장을 써 보세요.

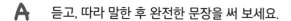

1 Social studies is + my favorite subject.

2 I am + really curious.

3 I like to + learn about cultures and societies.

4 Music is + my favorite subject.

5 I am + really joyful.

6 I like to + play the piano.

B 듣고, 문장의 빈칸을 채운 후 전체 문장을 다시 써 보세요.

1 _____ is my favorite subject. ⇨

2 Music is my _____. ⇨

3 _____ really curious. ⇨

4 I ____ really ____. ⇨

5 I ____ learn about cultures and societies. ⇨

6 I ____ the piano. ⇨

A 주어진 말을 바르게 배열해 문장을 완성하세요. 듣고, 문장 확인 후 뜻을 써 보세요.

1 is / Art / my favorite subject ⇨ _____

2 I / really creative / am ⇨ _____

3 like to / I / draw pictures ⇨ _____

4 is / my favorite subject / English ⇨ _____

5 am / I / really talkative ⇨ _____

6 like to / in English / I / talk with friends ⇨ _____

New Words art 미술 I creative 창의적인 I draw a picture 그림을 그리다

B 그림을 보고, 주어진 단어를 이용해 문장을 써 보세요.

수학은 내가 가장
좋아하는 과목이에요.
나는 정말 똑똑해요.
나는 수학 문제 푸는 걸 좋아해요.

_____

_____

_____

math 수학   solve 풀다   problem 문제

CHECK! CHECK! ☐ 첫 글자는 대문자로 썼나요?   ☐ 구두점은 찍었나요?   ☐ 단어와 단어 사이는 띄어 썼나요?

Unit 05 My Favorite Holiday 내가 가장 좋아하는 휴일

086

Read to Write

1. **Christmas is** a happy day. [주제]
크리스마스는 행복한 날이에요.

2. **I get** many presents. 나는 많은 선물을 받아요. [세부사항 1]

3. **I feel** happy. 나는 행복해요. [세부사항 2]

Step 0 패턴 이해하기

1. 어떤 휴일인가요? ⇨ **Christmas is** + a happy day.
happy는 '행복한'이라는 뜻으로 a happy day는 '행복한 날'이라는 의미예요. 이렇게 형용사(happy)는 명사(day)를 앞에서 꾸며 줘요.

2. 무슨 일이 있나요? ⇨ **I get** + many presents.
get은 '~을 받다'라는 의미이고, present는 '선물'이란 뜻이에요.

3. 기분이 어떤가요? ⇨ **I feel** + happy.
'feel + 형용사'는 '기분이 ~하다'라는 의미예요. feel 다음에 기분을 나타내는 형용사를 넣어 기분을 표현할 수 있어요.

087

Step 1 표현 파악하기 듣고, 따라 말해 보세요.

1.
Halloween / exciting
핼러윈 / 신나는
⇩

2.
wear a costume like a movie star
영화배우처럼 의상을 입다
⇩

3.
excited
신이 난

4.
New Year's Day / joyful
새해 첫날 / 기쁜, 즐거운
⇩

5.
watch a parade
퍼레이드를 보다
⇩

6.
great
멋진

A 듣고, 따라 말한 후 완전한 문장을 써 보세요.

1   Halloween is   +   an exciting day.

2   I wear   +   a costume like a movie star.

3   I feel   +   excited.

4   New Year's Day is +   a joyful day.

5   I watch   +   a parade.

6   I feel   +   great.

B 듣고, 문장의 빈칸을 채운 후 전체 문장을 다시 써 보세요.

1   _____ an exciting day.   ⇨

2   New Year's Day _____ day.   ⇨

3   _____ a costume like a movie star.   ⇨

4   I _____ .   ⇨

5   I _____ .   ⇨

6   _____ .   ⇨

A 주어진 말을 바르게 배열해 문장을 완성하세요. 듣고, 문장 확인 후 뜻을 써 보세요.

1 is / Valentine's Day /
   a wonderful day   ⇨ ....

2 exchange / I / cards and gifts /   ⇨ ....
   with friends

3 I / excited / feel   ⇨ ....

4 is / a great day / Thanksgiving Day ⇨ ....

5 with my family / delicious dishes /   ⇨ ....
   share / I

6 feel / warm and grateful / I   ⇨ ....

(New Words) exchange 교환하다 I delicious dishes 맛있는 음식들 I share 공유하다 I grateful 감사하는

B 그림을 보고, 주어진 단어를 이용해 문장을 써 보세요.

어머니의 날은 특별한 날이에요.
나는 엄마에게 선물들을 드려요.
나는 감사함과 행복을 느껴요.

....

....

....

Mother's Day 어머니의 날   special 특별한   give 주다   gift 선물

CHECK!
CHECK!   ☐ 첫 글자는 대문자로 썼나요?   ☐ 구두점은 찍었나요?   ☐ 단어와 단어 사이는 띄어 썼나요?

A   우리말에 맞게 빈칸에 알맞은 단어를 골라 써 보세요.

1   체육은 내가 가장 좋아하는 과목이에요. 나는 아주 활동적이에요.

_____ is my favorite subject. I am really _____.
　　　Art / P.E.　　　　　　　　　　　　　　　　curious / energetic

2   크리스마스는 행복한 날이에요. 나는 많은 선물을 받아요.

Christmas is a _____ day. I _____ many presents.
　　　　　　hungry / happy　　　　　give / get

3   그는 용감하고 친절해요. 그는 벽과 빌딩을 오를 수 있어요.

He is _____. He can _____ walls and buildings.
　　　brave and kind / shy and quiet　　　crawl / climb

B   질문에 알맞은 답을 <보기>에서 골라 써 보세요.

1   Who is your favorite friend?　　⇨

당신이 가장 좋아하는 친구는 누구인가요?

2   What does it taste like?　　⇨

그것은 어떤 맛인가요?

3   What can he do?　　⇨

그는 무엇을 할 수 있나요?

4   What do you like to do?　　⇨

당신은 무엇을 하는 것을 좋아하나요?

5   How do you feel?　　⇨

당신은 기분이 어떤가요?

보기

I feel happy.　　　It is super sweet.　　　I like to play soccer.
He can run faster than lightning.　　　My favorite friend is Ben.

C 주어진 말을 바르게 배열해 완전한 문장을 써 보세요.

1 kind-hearted / She / is ⇨

2 is / Supergirl / My favorite superhero ⇨

3 really creative / I / am ⇨

4 smash / He / bad men / can ⇨

5 a parade / watch / I ⇨

6 Halloween / an exciting day / is ⇨

D 문장을 보고, <u>틀린</u> 부분을 알맞게 고쳐 보세요.

1 i gives gifts To Mom. ⇨

나는 엄마에게 선물들을 드려요.

2 He am strong And cool. ⇨

그는 강하고 멋져요.

3 there is many Ingredients. ⇨

많은 재료가 (들어) 있어요.

4 I likes to Solve math problems. ⇨

나는 수학 문제를 푸는 걸 좋아해요.

5 she cans Fly in the sky. ⇨

그녀는 하늘을 날 수 있어요.

6 we both likes to plays computer games. ⇨

우리는 둘 다 컴퓨터 게임 하는 걸 좋아해요.

091

Read to Write

1 **I like** the marathon **the most.**　　　　[주제]
나는 마라톤을 가장 좋아해요.

2 **I learn** patience **from** running the marathon.　[세부사항 1]
나는 마라톤을 뛰면서 참을성을 배워요.

3 **What a** challenging sport! 정말 도전적인 운동이에요!　[세부사항 2]

Step 0　패턴 이해하기

1 가장 좋아하는 스포츠는
무엇인가요?
⇨ **I like** + the marathon + **the most.**
I like ~ the most는 '나는 ~을 가장 좋아한다'라는 의미예요.

2 그것에서 무엇을 배우나요?
⇨ **I learn** + patience + **from** running the marathon.
learn *A* from *B*는 'B에서 A를 배우다'라는 의미예요.

3 감탄스러운 점은 무엇인가요?
⇨ **What a** + challenging sport!
'What a(n) + 형용사 + 명사!'는 '정말 ~구나!'라는 의미로, 감탄을 나타내는 문장이에요.

092

Step 1　표현 파악하기　듣고, 따라 말해 보세요.

1
soccer
축구
⇩

2
teamwork
팀워크
⇩

3
passionate
열정적인

4
swimming
수영
⇩

5
confidence
자신감
⇩

6
incredible
놀라운

A　듣고, 따라 말한 후 완전한 문장을 써 보세요.

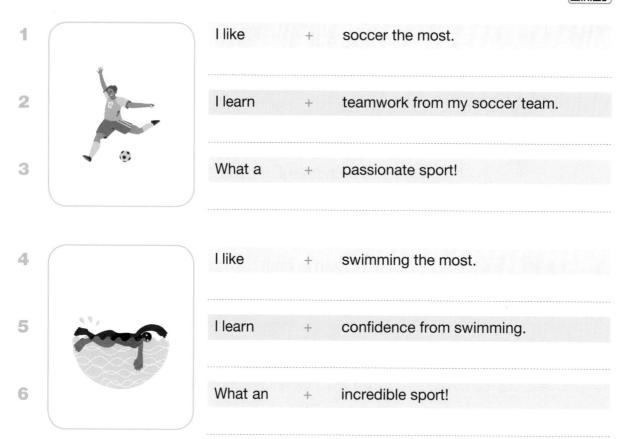

1	I like	+	soccer the most.
2	I learn	+	teamwork from my soccer team.
3	What a	+	passionate sport!

4	I like	+	swimming the most.
5	I learn	+	confidence from swimming.
6	What an	+	incredible sport!

B　듣고, 문장의 빈칸을 채운 후 전체 문장을 다시 써 보세요.

1 _____ soccer the most.　⇨

2 I _____ swimming _____ .　⇨

3 I _____ from my soccer team.　⇨

4 I _____ confidence _____ swimming.　⇨

5 _____ passionate sport!　⇨

6 _____ !　⇨

A 주어진 말을 바르게 배열해 문장을 완성하세요. 듣고, 문장 확인 후 뜻을 써 보세요.

1 like / I / figure skating / the most ⇨ _____

_____

2 I / balance / learn / from figure skating ⇨ _____

_____

3 a / skillful / What / sport! ⇨ _____

_____

4 the most / like / baseball / I ⇨ _____

_____

5 I / from my baseball team / teamwork / learn ⇨ _____

_____

6 What / cheerful / a / sport! ⇨ _____

_____

(New Words) figure skating 피겨 스케이팅 ǀ balance 균형 ǀ skillful 기술의 ǀ cheerful 쾌활한

B 그림을 보고, 주어진 단어를 이용해 문장을 써 보세요.

나는 배구를 가장 좋아해요.
저는 배구팀에서 팀워크를 배워요.
정말 신나는 스포츠예요!

_____

_____

_____

volleyball 배구   exciting 신나는   sport 스포츠, 운동

CHECK! CHECK! ☐ 첫 글자는 대문자로 썼나요?   ☐ 구두점은 찍었나요?   ☐ 단어와 단어 사이는 띄어 썼나요?

My Favorite Season and Weather

내가 가장 좋아하는 계절과 날씨

Read to Write

① **I think that** spring **is the best**. 나는 봄이 최고라고 생각해요. [주제]

② **It is** warm and breezy. 따뜻하고 바람이 솔솔 불어요. [세부사항 1]

③ **It is good for** enjoying outdoors. [세부사항 2]
야외 활동을 즐기기에 좋아요.

Step 0 패턴 이해하기

① 최고의 계절은 언제인가요? ⇨ **I think that** + spring + **is the best**.

I think that ~ is the best는 '나는 ~이 최고라고 생각한다'라는 의미예요.

② 날씨는 어떤가요? ⇨ **It is** + warm and breezy.

'It is + 날씨를 나타내는 단어'는 '날씨가 ~하다'라는 의미예요. 날씨를 나타낼 때는
주어를 It을 써요.

③ 무엇을 하기에 좋나요? ⇨ **It is good for** + enjoying outdoors.

It is good for ~는 '그것은 ~하기에 좋다'라는 의미예요. for 뒤에 동사가 올 때는
-ing 형태가 오기 때문에 enjoying으로 썼어요.

Step 1 표현 파악하기 듣고, 따라 말해 보세요.

1 summer 여름
⇩
2 hot and humid 덥고 습한
⇩
3 go to the beach 바닷가에 가다

4 fall 가을
⇩
5 cool and windy 시원하고 바람 부는
⇩
6 take a walk 산책하다

A 듣고, 따라 말한 후 완전한 문장을 써 보세요.

1	I think that	+	summer is the best.
2	It is	+	hot and humid.
3	It is good for	+	going to the beach.

4	I think that	+	fall is the best.
5	It is	+	cool and windy.
6	It is good for	+	taking a walk.

B 듣고, 문장의 빈칸을 채운 후 전체 문장을 다시 써 보세요.

1 _____ summer is the best. ⇨

2 I _____ is the best. ⇨

3 _____ and humid. ⇨

4 It _____ and _____ . ⇨

5 _____ for going to the beach. ⇨

6 It _____ a walk. ⇨

A 주어진 말을 바르게 배열해 문장을 완성하세요. 듣고, 문장 확인 후 뜻을 써 보세요.

1 that / think / winter is the best / I ⇨

_____

2 is / It / cold and dry ⇨

_____

3 It / good for / is / skiing and skating ⇨

_____

4 think / I / sunny weather is the best / that ⇨

_____

5 is / pleasant and bright / It ⇨

_____

6 is / good for / It / having a picnic ⇨

_____

(New Words) dry 건조한 I ski 스키를 타다 I skate 스케이트를 타다 I pleasant 쾌적한 I bright 밝은 I have a picnic 피크닉을 하다

B 그림을 보고, 주어진 단어와 표현을 이용해 문장을 써 보세요.

나는 눈 오는 날씨가
최고인 거 같아요.
눈이 오고 추워요.
눈사람 만들기에 좋아요.

_____

_____

_____

snowy 눈이 오는   make a snowman 눈사람을 만들다

CHECK!
CHECK!   ☐ 첫 글자는 대문자로 썼나요?   ☐ 구두점은 찍었나요?   ☐ 단어와 단어 사이는 띄어 썼나요?

Read to Write

101

1 **My favorite day of the week is** Tuesday. [주제]
내가 가장 좋아하는 요일은 화요일이에요.

2 **I have** art class **on** Tuesday**s**. [세부사항 1]
나는 화요일마다 미술 수업이 있어요.

3 **Drawing pictures is** really enjoyable. [세부사항 2]
그림을 그리는 것은 정말 즐거워요.

Step 0 **패턴 이해하기**

1 어떤 요일을 가장 좋아하나요? ⇨ **My favorite day of the week is** + Tuesday.

My favorite day of the week is ~는 '내가 가장 좋아하는 요일은 ~이다'라는 의미예요.

2 무슨 수업이 있나요? ⇨ **I have** + art class + **on** Tuesday**s**.

'have + 과목명'은 '~ 수업이 있다'란 뜻이에요. on Tuesdays는 '화요일마다'라는 뜻으로, 여러 번의 화요일이므로 Tuesdays라고 복수로 써요.

3 이유는 무엇인가요? ⇨ **Drawing pictures is** + really enjoyable.

drawing은 동사 draw에 -ing를 붙여 만든 동명사예요.

Step 1 **표현 파악하기** 듣고, 따라 말해 보세요.

102

1
Monday
월요일
⇩

2
English class
영어 수업
⇩

3
speak English / fun
영어로 말하다 / 재미있는

4
Wednesday
수요일
⇩

5
P.E. class
체육 수업
⇩

6
play sports / exciting
운동을 하다 / 신나는

A 듣고, 따라 말한 후 완전한 문장을 써 보세요.

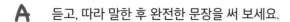

1 | My favorite day of the week is | + | Monday.

2 | I have English class | + | on Mondays.

3 | Speaking English is | + | really fun.

4 | My favorite day of the week is | + | Wednesday.

5 | I have P.E. class | + | on Wednesdays.

6 | Playing sports is | + | really exciting.

B 듣고, 문장의 빈칸을 채운 후 전체 문장을 다시 써 보세요.

1 My _____ of the week is Monday. ⇨

2 My favorite _____ of the _____ is Wednesday. ⇨

3 I _____ class on Mondays. ⇨

4 I _____ class _____ Wednesdays. ⇨

5 _____ really fun. ⇨

6 _____ is really _____. ⇨

A 주어진 말을 바르게 배열해 문장을 완성하세요. 듣고, 문장 확인 후 뜻을 써 보세요.

1 of the week / My favorite day / Thursday / is ⇨

----

2 I / a special cooking class / on Thursdays / have ⇨

----

3 Making dessert / really enjoyable / is ⇨

----

4 of the week / is / Wednesday / My favorite day ⇨

----

5 have / robot class / I / on Wednesdays ⇨

----

6 is / Making a robot / really interesting ⇨

(New Words) cooking class 요리 수업 ǀ make dessert 디저트를 만들다 ǀ enjoyable 즐거운 ǀ robot class 로봇 수업

B 그림을 보고, 주어진 단어와 표현을 이용해 문장을 써 보세요.

내가 가장 좋아하는 요일은
토요일이에요.
토요일마다 수업이 없어요.
늦게까지 자는 것은 정말 편해요.

----

have no class 수업이 없다 **sleep late** 늦게까지 자다 **relaxing** 편한

 CHECK! CHECK! ☐ 첫 글자는 대문자로 썼나요? ☐ 구두점은 찍었나요? ☐ 단어와 단어 사이는 띄어 썼나요?

Unit 09 The Best Thing About Vacation
방학의 가장 좋은 점

106

Read to Write

① **Summer vacation was** super fun.　　　[주제]
여름 방학은 정말 재미있었어요.

② **I went to** my grandma's house.　　　[세부사항 1]
나는 할머니 댁에 방문했어요.

③ **I enjoyed** swimm**ing** in the sea.　　　[세부사항 2]
나는 바다에서 수영을 즐겼어요.

Step 0　패턴 이해하기

① 방학은 어땠나요?　⇒ **Summer vacation was** + super fun.
super는 '대단히'라는 뜻으로, super fun은 '아주 재미있는'이라는 의미예요.
was는 be의 과거형으로 '~이었다, ~했다'라는 뜻이에요.

② 무엇을 했나요?　⇒ **I went to** + my grandma's house.
went는 go의 과거형으로, went to는 '~에 갔다'라는 의미예요.

③ 무엇을 즐겼나요?　⇒ **I enjoyed** swimm**ing** + in the sea.
'I enjoyed + 동사-ing'는 '나는 ~하는 것을 즐겼다'라는 의미예요.

Step 1　표현 파악하기　듣고, 따라 말해 보세요.

107

| 1 | spring vacation 봄 방학 | 4 | winter vacation 겨울 방학 |

⇩ ⇩

| 2 | the festival 축제 | 5 | the ski resort 스키 리조트 |

⇩ ⇩

| 3 | watch the parade 퍼레이드를 보다 | 6 | ski all day 하루 종일 스키를 타다 |

A 듣고, 따라 말한 후 완전한 문장을 써 보세요.

1 | Spring vacation was | + | super fun.

2  | I went to | + | the festival.

3 | I enjoyed | + | watching the parade.

4 | Winter vacation was | + | super fun.

5 | I went to | + | the ski resort.

6 | I enjoyed | + | skiing all day.

B 듣고, 문장의 빈칸을 채운 후 전체 문장을 다시 써 보세요.

1 _____ was super fun. ⇨

2 Winter _____ fun. ⇨

3 _____ the festival. ⇨

4 I _____ ski resort. ⇨

5 _____ the parade. ⇨

6 _____ all day. ⇨

A 주어진 말을 바르게 배열해 문장을 완성하세요. 듣고, 문장 확인 후 뜻을 써 보세요.

110

1 was / super fun / Summer vacation ⇨

2 the pool / I / went to ⇨

3 I / eating / ice cream / enjoyed ⇨

4 Spring vacation / super fun / was ⇨

5 went to / the park / I ⇨

6 enjoyed / I / beautiful flowers / seeing ⇨

New Words   summer vacation 여름 방학 I see 보다

B 그림을 보고, 주어진 표현을 이용해 문장을 써 보세요.

겨울 방학이 정말 재미있었어요.
나는 공원에 갔어요.
나는 눈싸움하는 것을 즐겼어요.

go to the park 공원에 가다   **have a snowball fight** 눈싸움을 하다

CHECK!
CHECK!   ☐ 첫 글자는 대문자로 썼나요?   ☐ 구두점은 찍었나요?   ☐ 단어와 단어 사이는 띄어 썼나요?

A 우리말에 맞게 빈칸에 알맞은 단어를 골라 써 보세요.

1 나는 눈 오는 날씨가 최고인 거 같아요. 눈사람 만들기에 좋아요.

I think _____ weather is the best. It is good for _____ a snowman.
snowy / sunny   having / making

2 나는 수요일마다 체육 수업이 있어요. 운동을 하는 것은 너무 신나요.

I have _____ class on Wednesdays. Playing sports is really _____.
P.E. / music   difficult / exciting

3 나는 스키 리조트에 갔어요. 나는 스키를 하루 종일 즐겼어요.

I went to the _____. I enjoyed _____ all day.
ski resort / festival   watching / skiing

B 질문에 알맞은 답을 <보기>에서 골라 써 보세요.

1 What is your favorite sport?   ⇨

당신은 무슨 스포츠를 가장 좋아하나요?

2 What is the weather like?   ⇨

날씨가 어떤가요?

3 What class do you have on Tuesdays? ⇨

화요일마다 무슨 수업이 있어요?

4 Where did you go?   ⇨

당신은 어디에 갔었나요?

5 How was summer vacation?   ⇨

여름 방학은 어땠나요?

보기

I went to my grandma's house.   Summer vacation was super fun.
It is warm and breezy.   I have art class on Tuesdays.   I like the marathon the most.

C 주어진 말을 바르게 배열해 완전한 문장을 써 보세요.

1 enjoyed / I / eating ice cream ⇨

2 have robot class / on Wednesdays / I ⇨

3 really relaxing / is / Sleeping late ⇨

4 pleasant and bright / is / It ⇨

5 an exciting / What / sport! ⇨

6 learn / teamwork / I / from my soccer team ⇨

D 문장을 보고, 틀린 부분을 알맞게 고쳐 보세요.

1 it am Good for enjoying outdoors. ⇨

날이 야외 활동을 즐기기에 좋아요.

2 My favorite day of the week are monday. ⇨

내가 가장 좋아하는 요일은 월요일이에요.

3 winter vacation were Super fun. ⇨

겨울 방학은 정말 재미있었어요.

4 drawing pictures are really Enjoyable. ⇨

그림을 그리는 것은 정말 즐거워요.

5 i thinks that sunny weather is the Best. ⇨

나는 화창한 날씨가 최고라고 생각해요.

6 I liked Baseball the most. ⇨

나는 야구를 가장 좋아해요.

Unit 10 The Best Place in the City
도시에서 최고의 장소

Read to Write

1 Happy Shopping Mall is **the best place in my city**. [주제]
행복쇼핑몰은 우리 도시에서 최고의 장소예요.

2 **It has** many restaurants. 그곳에는 많은 식당이 있어요. [세부사항 1]

3 **I can eat** delicious food there. [세부사항 2]
나는 거기에서 맛있는 음식을 먹을 수 있어요.

Step 0 패턴 이해하기

1 도시에서 최고의 장소는
어디인가요?
⇨ Happy Shopping Mall is + **the best place in my city**.
the best는 '최고의'라는 뜻으로, the best place in my city는 '우리 도시 최고의 장소'라는 의미예요.

2 그곳에는 무엇이 있나요?
⇨ **It has** + many restaurants.
restaurant는 '식당'이란 뜻이고, have many restaurants는 '많은 식당이 있다'란 말이에요. 주어가 It이어서 has를 썼어요.

3 무엇을 할 수 있나요?
⇨ **I can eat** + delicious food there.
'I can + 동사원형'은 '나는 ~할 수 있다'라는 의미예요.

Step 1 표현 파악하기 듣고, 따라 말해 보세요.

1
Fun Toy Store
펀 장난감 가게
⇩

2
interesting toys
흥미로운 장난감들
⇩

3
hold and play with them
그것들을 가지고 놀다

4
Nari Tower
나리 타워
⇩

5
an observation deck
전망대
⇩

6
enjoy the city view at a glance
한눈에 도시 경관을 즐기다

Step 2 패턴 문장 뼈대 잡기

A 듣고, 따라 말한 후 완전한 문장을 써 보세요.

1 Fun Toy Store is   +   the best place in my city.

2 It has   +   interesting toys.

3 I can hold and play   +   with them.

4 Nari Tower is   +   the best place in my city.

5 It has   +   an observation deck.

6 I can enjoy   +   the city view at a glance.

B 듣고, 문장의 빈칸을 채운 후 전체 문장을 다시 써 보세요.

1 Fun Toy Store is _____ place in my city. ⇨

2 Nari Tower is _____ in my city. ⇨

3 _____ interesting _____ . ⇨

4 It _____ . ⇨

5 _____ and play with them. ⇨

6 I _____ the city view at a glance. ⇨

Step 3 패턴 문장 만들기

A 주어진 말을 바르게 배열해 문장을 완성하세요. 듣고, 문장 확인 후 뜻을 써 보세요.

115

1 is / the best place in my city / The National Museum ⇨

2 has / It / many exhibitions ⇨

3 I / pictures and sculptures / can / look at ⇨

4 is / in my city / the best place / The dog park ⇨

5 It / a large playground / has ⇨

6 with my dog / play / can / I ⇨

New Words   National Museum 국립박물관 ㅣ exhibition 전시회 ㅣ sculpture 조각

B 그림을 보고, 주어진 단어를 이용해 문장을 써 보세요.

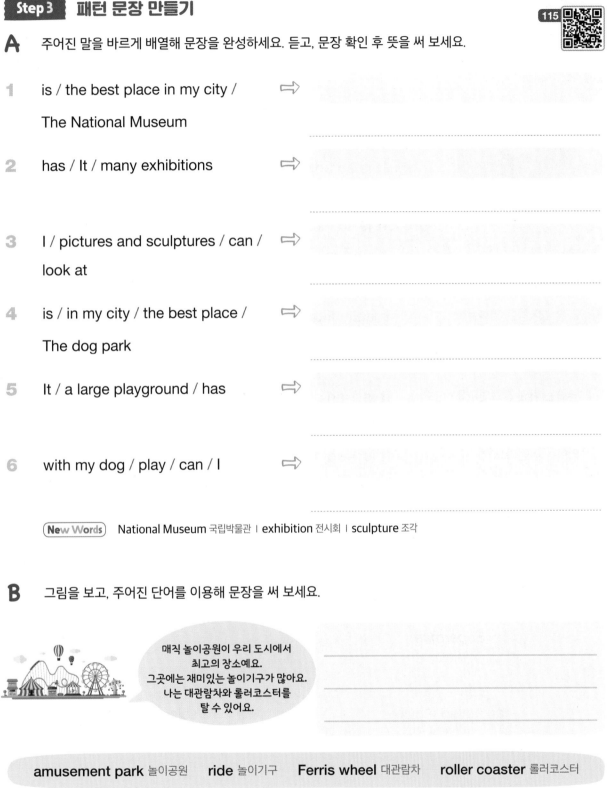

매직 놀이공원이 우리 도시에서
최고의 장소예요.
그곳에는 재미있는 놀이기구가 많아요.
나는 대관람차와 롤러코스터를
탈 수 있어요.

amusement park 놀이공원   ride 놀이기구   Ferris wheel 대관람차   roller coaster 롤러코스터

CHECK!
CHECK!   ☐ 첫 글자는 대문자로 썼나요?   ☐ 구두점은 찍었나요?   ☐ 단어와 단어 사이는 띄어 썼나요?

Read to Write

① **I really like** *Zootopia*. [주제]
나는 <주토피아>를 정말 좋아해요.

② **It is** an animated movie. [세부사항 1]
그것은 애니메이션 영화예요.

③ **It is** so exciting. 그것은 정말 신나요. [세부사항 2]

Step 0 패턴 이해하기

① 가장 좋아하는 영화는
무엇인가요?

⇒ **I really like** + *Zootopia*.

like는 '~을 좋아하다'라는 의미예요. 정말 좋아한다고 강조할 때 앞에 really를
붙여요.

② 영화는 어떤 장르인가요?

⇒ **It is** + an animated movie.

animated movie는 '애니메이션 영화'라는 의미예요.

③ 영화는 어떤가요?

⇒ **It is** + so exciting.

so는 '아주'라는 뜻으로, so exciting 하면 '아주 흥미로운'이라는 뜻이 되어
exciting의 의미가 강조돼요.

Step 1 표현 파악하기 듣고, 따라 말해 보세요.

1
Superman
슈퍼맨
⇩

4
Avatar
아바타
⇩

2
an action movie
액션 영화
⇩

5
a science fiction movie
공상 과학 영화
⇩

3
so thrilling
아주 짜릿한

6
so interesting
아주 흥미로운

A 듣고, 따라 말한 후 완전한 문장을 써 보세요.

1	I really like	+	*Superman*.
2	It is	+	an action movie.
3	It is	+	so thrilling.

4	I really like	+	*Avatar*.
5	It is	+	a science fiction movie.
6	It is	+	so interesting.

B 듣고, 문장의 빈칸을 채운 후 전체 문장을 다시 써 보세요.

1 I _____ *Superman*. ⇨

2 _____ *Avatar*. ⇨

3 _____ movie. ⇨

4 It is a _____ . ⇨

5 _____ thrilling. ⇨

6 It _____ . ⇨

A 주어진 말을 바르게 배열해 문장을 완성하세요. 듣고, 문장 확인 후 뜻을 써 보세요.

1 like / I / *Hidden Figures* / really ⇨

2 is / It / a history movie ⇨

3 is / so touching / It ⇨

4 like / I / really / *Up* ⇨

5 is / an animated movie / It ⇨

6 is / It / so sad ⇨

(New Words) history movie 역사 영화 ǀ touching 감동적인

B 그림을 보고, 주어진 단어를 이용해 문장을 써 보세요.

나는 <마틸다(Matilda)>를 정말 좋아해요.
그것은 뮤지컬 영화예요.
그것은 정말 신나요.

musical movie 뮤지컬 영화   **exciting** 신나는

CHECK! CHECK!   ☐ 첫 글자는 대문자로 썼나요?   ☐ 구두점은 찍었나요?   ☐ 단어와 단어 사이는 띄어 썼나요?

121

Read to Write

1 **The perfect pet for me is** a dog.　　[주제]
나에게 딱 맞는 반려동물은 개예요.

2 **Dogs are** incredibly loyal.　　[세부사항 1]
개들은 믿을 수 없을 만큼 충성스러워요.

3 **I smile** when they wag their tails.　　[세부사항 2]
개들이 꼬리를 흔들면 나는 미소를 지어요.

Step 0　패턴 이해하기

1 어떤 반려동물이 가장 완벽한가요?　⇨　**The perfect pet for me is** + a dog.

the perfect pet for me는 '나에게 가장 딱 맞는 반려동물'이라는 뜻이에요.

2 그것은 어떤 특징이 있나요?　⇨　**Dogs are** + incredibly loyal.

Dogs are ~는 '개들은 ~이다'라는 뜻이에요.

3 반려동물이 좋을 때는 언제인가요?　⇨　**I smile** + when they wag their tails.

when은 '~할 때'라는 뜻으로, when they wag their tails는 '그들이(개들이)
꼬리를 흔들 때'라는 의미예요. when은 어떤 일이 발생하는 시점을 나타내요.

122

Step 1　표현 파악하기　　듣고, 따라 말해 보세요.

1
a cat
고양이
⇩

2
playful / independent
장난기 많은 / 독립적인
⇩

3
smile / hug
미소 짓다 / 껴안다

4
a hamster
햄스터
⇩

5
adorable
사랑스러운
⇩

6
laugh / play in a cage
웃다 / 우리에서 놀다

A 듣고, 따라 말한 후 완전한 문장을 써 보세요.

1   The perfect pet for me is   +   a cat.

2   Cats are   +   playful and independent.

3   I smile   +   when they hug me.

4   The perfect pet for me is   +   a hamster.

5   Hamsters are   +   so adorable.

6   I laugh   +   when they play in a cage.

B 듣고, 문장의 빈칸을 채운 후 전체 문장을 다시 써 보세요.

1   ＿＿＿＿＿＿＿＿＿＿ for me is a cat.   ⇨

2   The perfect ＿＿＿ for me ＿＿＿ a hamster.   ⇨

3   ＿＿＿＿＿＿＿＿＿＿ and independent.   ⇨

4   Hamsters ＿＿＿＿＿＿＿＿＿＿.   ⇨

5   ＿＿＿＿＿＿＿＿＿＿ they hug me.   ⇨

6   I laugh ＿＿＿ they ＿＿＿ in a cage.   ⇨

A 주어진 말을 바르게 배열해 문장을 완성하세요. 듣고, 문장 확인 후 뜻을 써 보세요.

1 for me / is a rabbit / The perfect pet ⇨

----

2 are / Rabbits / adorable and fluffy ⇨

----

3 smile / I / when they hop ⇨

----

4 for me / is / The perfect pet / a fish ⇨

----

5 are / Fish / incredibly beautiful ⇨

----

6 smile / when they swim gracefully / I ⇨

(New Words) fluffy 솜털로 뒤덮인 ǀ incredibly 믿을 수 없을 만큼, 엄청나게 ǀ gracefully 우아하게

B 그림을 보고, 주어진 단어를 이용해 문장을 써 보세요.

나에게 딱 맞는 반려동물은 고슴도치예요. 고슴도치들은 믿을 수 없을 만큼 귀여워요. 나는 그들이 우리에서 탐험을 할 때 미소를 지어요.

----

hedgehog 고슴도치 **explore** 탐험하다

CHECK! CHECK! ☐ 첫 글자는 대문자로 썼나요? ☐ 구두점은 찍었나요? ☐ 단어와 단어 사이는 띄어 썼나요?

Read to Write

① **I really love** the Italian restaurant.　　　[주제]
나는 그 이탈리아 식당을 아주 좋아해요.

② **It is famous for** its seafood pizza.　　　[세부사항 1]
그 식당은 해산물 피자로 유명해요.

③ **The pizza is** really fresh and delicious.　　　[세부사항 2]
그 피자는 정말 신선하고 맛있어요.

Step 0 패턴 이해하기

① 어느 식당을 가장 좋아하나요?　⇒ **I really love** + the Italian restaurant.
I really love ~는 '나는 ~을 아주 좋아한다'란 의미예요.

② 어떤 음식이 유명한가요?　⇒ **It is famous for** + its seafood pizza.
be famous for는 '~로 유명하다'란 의미예요.

③ 그 음식의 특징은 무엇인가요?　⇒ **The pizza is** + really fresh and delicious.
really는 '정말', fresh and delicious는 '신선하고 맛있는'이란 의미예요.

Step 1 표현 파악하기　듣고, 따라 말해 보세요.

1
| the Chinese restaurant |
| 중식당 |
⇩

2
| dim sum |
| 딤섬 |
⇩

3
| juicy and tasty |
| 즙이 많고 맛있는 |

4
| the Japanese restaurant |
| 일식당 |
⇩

5
| sushi |
| 스시 |
⇩

6
| fresh and healthy |
| 신선하고 건강에 좋은 |

A 듣고, 따라 말한 후 완전한 문장을 써 보세요.

1   I really love   +   the Chinese restaurant.

2   It is famous for   +   its dim sum.

3   The dim sum is   +   really juicy and tasty.

4   I really love   +   the Japanese restaurant.

5   It is famous for   +   its sushi.

6   The sushi is   +   really fresh and healthy.

B 듣고, 문장의 빈칸을 채운 후 전체 문장을 다시 써 보세요.

1   _____ the Chinese restaurant. ⇨

2   I _____ Japanese restaurant. ⇨

3   _____ for its dim sum. ⇨

4   It _____ sushi. ⇨

5   _____ is really juicy and tasty. ⇨

6   The sushi is _____ and healthy. ⇨

A 주어진 말을 바르게 배열해 문장을 완성하세요. 듣고, 문장 확인 후 뜻을 써 보세요.

1 really love / the chicken restaurant / I   ⇨

_____

2 It / its fried chicken / is famous for   ⇨

_____

3 is / crispy and chewy / really /   ⇨

The fried chicken

_____

4 really love / I / the Indian restaurant   ⇨

_____

5 is famous for / It / its beef curry   ⇨

_____

6 The beef curry / spicy and yummy /   ⇨

is / really

_____

(New Words) chicken 치킨 | crispy 바삭한 | chewy 쫄깃한 | Indian 인도의 | beef curry 소고기 커리 | spicy 매운

B 그림을 보고, 주어진 단어를 이용해 문장을 써 보세요.

나는 그 베트남 식당을 아주 좋아해요.
그곳은 쌀국수와 스프링롤로 유명해요.
그 쌀국수는 정말
건강에 좋고 맛있어요.

_____

_____

_____

Vietnamese 베트남의   pho 쌀국수   spring rolls 스프링롤

CHECK!
CHECK!   ☐ 첫 글자는 대문자로 썼나요?   ☐ 구두점은 찍었나요?   ☐ 단어와 단어 사이는 띄어 썼나요?

My Favorite Family Member

내가 가장 좋아하는 가족 구성원

 131

Read to Write

1 **My favorite family member is** my mom. [주제]

내가 가장 좋아하는 가족 구성원은 우리 엄마예요.

2 **She is** warm-hearted and bright. [세부사항 1]

그녀는 마음이 따뜻하고 밝아요.

3 **She always gives** me love. [세부사항 2]

그녀는 항상 나를 사랑해 줘요.

Step 0 패턴 이해하기

1 최고의 가족 구성원은 누구인가요?

⇨ **My favorite family member is** + my mom.

My favorite family member is ~는 '내가 가장 좋아하는 가족 구성원은 ~이다' 라는 의미예요.

2 어떤 사람인가요?

⇨ **She is** + warm-hearted and bright.

warm-hearted는 '마음이 따뜻한', bright는 '밝은'이라는 뜻이에요.

3 무엇을 해 주나요?

⇨ **She always gives** + me + love.

give A B는 'A에게 B를 주다'라는 의미예요.

Step 1 표현 파악하기 듣고, 따라 말해 보세요.

 132

1
dad
아빠
⇩

2
wise and strong
현명하고 강한
⇩

3
encourage me
나를 격려하다

4
grandmother
할머니
⇩

5
loving and caring
사랑이 많고 배려가 깊은
⇩

6
cook delicious food
맛있는 음식을 요리하다

A 듣고, 따라 말한 후 완전한 문장을 써 보세요.

1   My favorite family member is   +   my dad.

2   He is   +   wise and strong.

3   He always encourages   +   me.

4   My favorite family member is   +   my grandmother.

5   She is   +   loving and caring.

6   She always cooks   +   delicious food.

B 듣고, 문장의 빈칸을 채운 후 전체 문장을 다시 써 보세요.

1   _____ family member is my dad.   ⇨

2   My favorite _____ is my grandmother.   ⇨

3   _____ and strong.   ⇨

4   She _____ and caring.   ⇨

5   _____ always _____ .   ⇨

6   She always _____ food.   ⇨

A 주어진 말을 바르게 배열해 문장을 완성하세요. 듣고, 문장 확인 후 뜻을 써 보세요.

135

1 is / My favorite family member / my grandfather ⇨ _____

2 is / knowledgeable and wise / He ⇨ _____

3 always / answers / He / me ⇨ _____

4 is / My favorite family member / my sister ⇨ _____

5 is / kind and friendly / She ⇨ _____

6 me / always / She / supports ⇨ _____

(New Words) knowledgeable 아는 것이 많은 ǀ wise 현명한 ǀ answer 대답하다 ǀ friendly 다정한 ǀ support 응원하다

B 그림을 보고, 주어진 단어를 이용해 문장을 써 보세요.

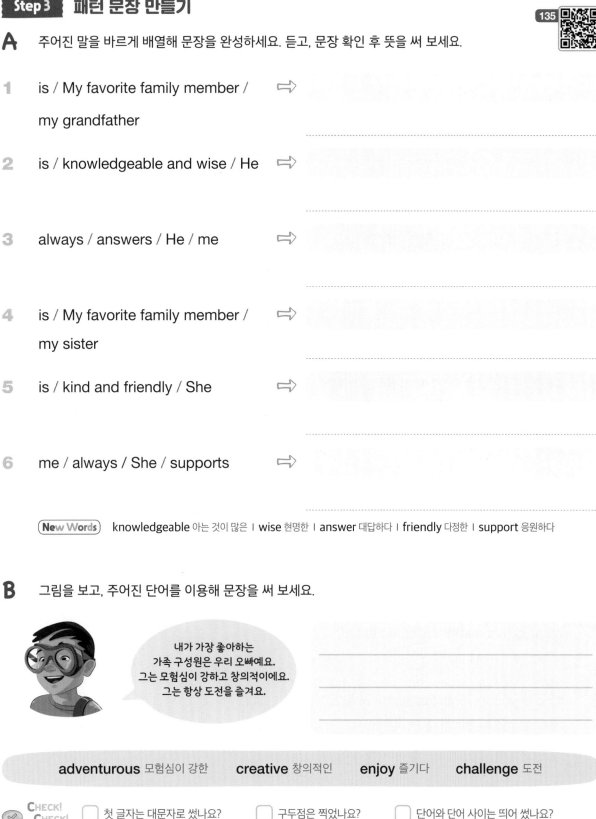

내가 가장 좋아하는 가족 구성원은 우리 오빠예요. 그는 모험심이 강하고 창의적이에요. 그는 항상 도전을 즐겨요.

adventurous 모험심이 강한   creative 창의적인   enjoy 즐기다   challenge 도전

CHECK! CHECK! ☐ 첫 글자는 대문자로 썼나요?   ☐ 구두점은 찍었나요?   ☐ 단어와 단어 사이는 띄어 썼나요?

A 우리말에 맞게 빈칸에 알맞은 단어를 골라 써 보세요.

1 나는 그 일식당을 좋아해요. 그 스시는 정말 신선하고 건강에 좋아요.

I really love the _____ restaurant. The sushi is really _____.

Chinese / Japanese   *fresh and healthy / juicy and tasty*

2 햄스터들은 너무 사랑스러워요. 나는 그들이 우리에서 놀 때 웃어요.

Hamsters are so _____. I laugh when they _____ in a cage.

playful / adorable   *play / hug*

3 나는 <슈퍼맨>을 정말 좋아해요. 그것은 아주 신이 나요.

I really like _____. It is so _____.

Avatar / Superman   *sad / thrilling*

B 질문에 알맞은 답을 <보기>에서 골라 써 보세요.

1 What is the best place in your city?   ⇨

당신 도시에서 최고의 장소는 어디인가요?

2 What kind of genre is the movie?   ⇨

그 영화는 어떤 장르인가요?

3 What pet is perfect for you?   ⇨

어떤 반려동물이 당신한테 가장 잘 맞나요?

4 What is this restaurant famous for? ⇨

이 식당은 뭘로 유명한가요?

5 Who is your favorite family member? ⇨

당신이 가장 좋아하는 가족 구성원은 누구인가요?

보기

The perfect pet for me is a dog.   It is an animated movie.
It is famous for its seafood pizza.   My favorite family member is my mom.
Happy Shopping Mall is the best place in my city.

C 주어진 말을 바르게 배열해 완전한 문장을 써 보세요.

1 has / a large playground / It ⇨

2 can / at a glance / enjoy the city view / I ⇨

3 really like / I / *Hidden Figures* ⇨

4 a history movie / is / It ⇨

5 incredibly loyal / are / Dogs ⇨

6 is famous for / It / its dim sum ⇨

D 문장을 보고, <u>틀린</u> 부분을 알맞게 고쳐 보세요.

1 nari Tower am the Best place In my City. ⇨
나리 타워는 우리 도시에서 최고의 장소예요.

2 It are So interesting. ⇨
그것은 정말 흥미로워요.

3 i smiled When they hug me. ⇨
그들이 나를 안아 줄 때 나는 미소를 지어요.

4 the Fried chicken am really crispy And chewy. ⇨
그 프라이드 치킨은 정말 바삭하고 쫄깃해요.

5 she are Loving and caring. ⇨
그녀는 사랑이 많고 배려가 깊어요.

6 she always enjoy cHallenges. ⇨
그는 항상 도전을 즐겨요.

PART 3

온라인 글쓰기
(문자 메시지, SNS, 채팅, 블로그, 홈페이지)

온라인 글쓰기는 블로그나 SNS 등에 정보를 제공하거나 나만의 생각을 표현하는 글쓰기입니다. 매일 쉽게 접할 수 있기 때문에 글쓰기를 연습하기에 좋습니다.

<온라인 글쓰기 방법>

1. 먼저 어떤 정보나 의견에 대해 쓸지 생각해 봅니다.
2. 주제를 정하고 나면 중요한 정보가 무엇인지 내 생각을 정리하여 적어 봅니다.
3. 쉽고 간단한 문장으로 전달하면 다른 사람과 소통하기가 더 쉬워집니다.

예를 들어, 잃어버린 반려동물을 찾는 글을 쓴다면 그 동물을 잃어버린 장소, 동물의 특징에 대해 적어 봅니다. 처음에는 글쓰기 가이드 질문에 대한 답을 적어 나가 보는 것도 괜찮습니다. 답을 적다 보면 어느새 온라인 글이 완성되고 글을 쓰는 감각도 길러집니다.

예시

주제	찾고 있는 동물은 무엇인가요?	I am looking for my cat.
세부사항 1	어디에서 잃어버렸나요?	I lost him in the park.
세부사항 2	어떻게 생겼나요?	He has white fur.

Unit 01 Invitation Messages 초대 메시지(문자 메시지)

Read to Write

① **What are you doing** this Saturday, Jane?　[주제]
제인아, 이번 주 토요일에 뭐 할 거야?

② **Let's have** a pajama party. 파자마 파티 하자.　[세부사항 1]

③ **We can have** fun together.　[세부사항 2]
우리는 함께 즐거운 시간을 보낼 수 있어.

Step 0　패턴 이해하기

① 친구의 일정을 물어볼까요?　⇒ **What are you doing** + this Saturday, Jane?
What are you doing?(뭐 하는 중이야?)을 this Saturday(이번 주 토요일에)
처럼 미래를 나타내는 말과 함께 쓰면 미래의 일정을 묻는 표현이 돼요.

② 무얼 하자고 할까요?　⇒ **Let's have** + a pajama party.
'Let's + 동사원형'은 '(함께) ~하자'라는 의미로 권유할 때 쓰는 표현이에요.
have a pajama party는 '파자마 파티를 하다'란 뜻이에요.

③ 거기서 무엇을 할 수 있나요?　⇒ **We can have** + fun together.
'We can + 동사원형'은 '우리는 ~할 수 있다'라는 의미예요. have fun은 '재미
있게 보내다'라는 의미예요.

Step 1　표현 파악하기　듣고, 따라 말해 보세요.

1
tomorrow
내일
⇩

2
go to the river
강에 가다
⇩

3
fish in the river
강에서 낚시하다

4
this Friday
이번 주 금요일
⇩

5
go to the zoo
동물원에 가다
⇩

6
see pandas
판다를 보다

A   듣고, 따라 말한 후 완전한 문장을 써 보세요.

1		What are you doing	+	tomorrow, Lora?
2		Let's go	+	to the river.
3		We can fish	+	in the river.

4		What are you doing	+	this Friday, Sarah?
5		Let's go	+	to the zoo.
6		We can see	+	pandas.

B   듣고, 문장의 빈칸을 채운 후 전체 문장을 다시 써 보세요.

1 _____ doing tomorrow, Lora? ⇨

2 What are you doing _____, Sarah? ⇨

3 _____ to the river. ⇨

4 Let's go _____ . ⇨

5 _____ in the river. ⇨

6 We _____ . ⇨

A 주어진 말을 바르게 배열해 문장을 완성하세요. 듣고, 문장 확인 후 뜻을 써 보세요.

1 are you / What / this Monday, / doing / Jin? ⇨

2 Let's go / the library / to ⇨

3 can read / We / new books ⇨

4 this Wednesday, / are you / Chris? / ⇨
   doing / What

5 the beach / go to / Let's ⇨

6 We / fireworks / can see ⇨

(New Words) firework 불꽃놀이

B 그림을 보고, 주어진 단어와 표현을 이용해 문장을 써 보세요.

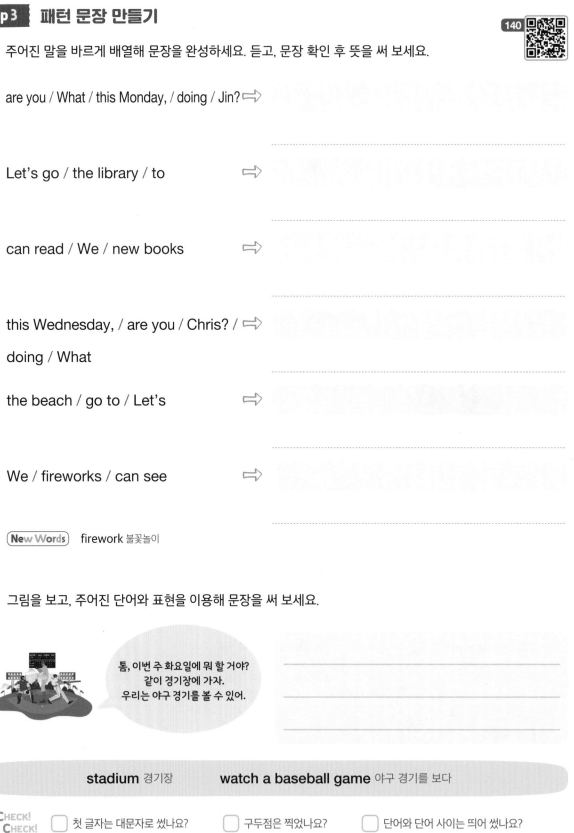

톰, 이번 주 화요일에 뭐 할 거야?
같이 경기장에 가자.
우리는 야구 경기를 볼 수 있어.

stadium 경기장   **watch a baseball game** 야구 경기를 보다

CHECK!
CHECK!   ☐ 첫 글자는 대문자로 썼나요?   ☐ 구두점은 찍었나요?   ☐ 단어와 단어 사이는 띄어 썼나요?

 141

Read to Write

1. **Thank you for** the dress, Aunt Grace. [주제]
   드레스 고맙습니다, 그레이스 이모.

2. **The dress is** really awesome. 그 드레스는 정말 멋져요. [세부사항 1]

3. **You are** so kind. 이모는 정말 친절하세요. [세부사항 2]

Step 0 패턴 이해하기

1 누구에게 무엇에 대해
  감사하고 있나요?
  ⇒ **Thank you for** + the dress, Aunt Grace.
  Thank you for ~는 '~에 대해 고맙습니다'라는 뜻이에요. 감사할 일이 있을 때 쓸
  수 있어요.

2 그 선물이 왜 좋았나요?
  ⇒ **The dress is** + really awesome.
  really awesome은 '정말 멋진'이란 뜻이에요. really(부사)는 awesome(형용사)
  앞에서 그 의미를 강조해 주고 있어요.

3 감사의 대상은 어떤가요?
  ⇒ **You are** + so kind.
  so는 '아주'라는 뜻으로, so kind는 '아주 친절한'이라는 의미예요.

 142

Step 1 표현 파악하기 듣고, 따라 말해 보세요.

1
the gloves / Uncle Tom
장갑 / 톰 삼촌
⇩

2
fantastic
환상적인
⇩

3
friendly
다정한

4
the cap / Mom
모자 / 엄마
⇩

5
terrific
멋진
⇩

6
awesome
굉장한

A 듣고, 따라 말한 후 완전한 문장을 써 보세요.

1 | Thank you for | + | the gloves, Uncle Tom.

2  | The gloves are | + | really fantastic.

3 | You are | + | so friendly.

4 | Thank you for | + | the cap, Mom.

5 | The cap is | + | really terrific.

6 | You are | + | so awesome.

B 듣고, 문장의 빈칸을 채운 후 전체 문장을 다시 써 보세요.

1 _____ for the gloves, Uncle Tom. ⇨

2 Thank you for _____ , _____ . ⇨

3 _____ really fantastic. ⇨

4 The cap _____ . ⇨

5 _____ friendly. ⇨

6 You _____ . ⇨

A 주어진 말을 바르게 배열해 문장을 완성하세요. 듣고, 문장 확인 후 뜻을 써 보세요.

145

1   the jeans, / Amy / Thank you for   ⇨

2   are / The jeans / really trendy   ⇨

3   are / You / so wonderful   ⇨

4   the jacket, / Leo / Thank you for   ⇨

5   is / The jacket / really pretty   ⇨

6   are / You / so nice   ⇨

New Words   trendy 최신 유행하는 I wonderful 멋있는 I jacket 재킷

B 그림을 보고, 주어진 단어를 이용해 문장을 써 보세요.

선글라스 고마워,
미구엘(Miguel).
그 선글라스는 정말 멋있어.
너는 정말 다정해.

sunglasses 선글라스   friendly 다정한

CHECK!
CHECK!   ☐ 첫 글자는 대문자로 썼나요?   ☐ 구두점은 찍었나요?   ☐ 단어와 단어 사이는 띄어 썼나요?

03 Looking for a Pet 잃어버린 반려동물 찾기(SNS)

Read to Write

1 **I am looking for** my dog, Toto. [주제]
나는 토토라는 내 강아지를 찾고 있어요.

2 **I lost her** in the park. 나는 공원에서 그것을 잃어버렸어요. [세부사항 1]

3 **She has** black fur. 그것은 털이 검은색이에요. [세부사항 2]

Step 0 패턴 이해하기

1 찾고 있는 반려동물의 이름은? ⇨ **I am looking for** + my dog, Toto.

I am looking for ~는 '나는 ~을 찾고 있는 중이다'란 의미예요. 이렇게 'be동사 + 동사-ing'는 현재 진행중인 일을 나타낼 때 써요.

2 어디에서 잃어버렸나요? ⇨ **I lost her** + in the park.

lost(잃어버렸다)는 동사 lose의 과거형이에요. in the park는 '공원에서'라는 뜻으로, in 뒤에 장소가 와요.

3 어떻게 생겼나요? ⇨ **She has** + black fur.

'털이 있다, 눈이 크다' 등 생김새를 나타낼 때 동사 have를 써요. 주어가 She/He/It이면 has를 써요.

Step 1 표현 파악하기 듣고, 따라 말해 보세요.

1
my cat, Molly
나의 고양이, 몰리
⇩

2
at the bus stop
버스 정류장에서
⇩

3
a long tail and big eyes
긴 꼬리와 큰 눈

4
my hamster, Tiny
나의 햄스터, 타이니
⇩

5
in this building
이 건물에서
⇩

6
red hair and black eyes
붉은 털과 검은색 눈

Step 2 패턴 문장 뼈대 잡기

A 듣고, 따라 말한 후 완전한 문장을 써 보세요.

1	I am looking for	+	my cat, Molly.
2	I lost her	+	at the bus stop.
3	She has	+	a long tail and big eyes.
4	I am looking for	+	my hamster, Tiny.
5	I lost him	+	in this building.
6	He has	+	red hair and black eyes.

B 듣고, 문장의 빈칸을 채운 후 전체 문장을 다시 써 보세요.

1 _____ for my cat, Molly. ⇨

2 I am looking for _____, Tiny. ⇨

3 _____ at the bus stop. ⇨

4 I _____ this building. ⇨

5 _____ long tail and big eyes. ⇨

6 He _____ and black eyes. ⇨

A 주어진 말을 바르게 배열해 문장을 완성하세요. 듣고, 문장 확인 후 뜻을 써 보세요.

150

1 am looking for / I / my rabbit, / Bunny ⇨

_____

2 in the mall / I / her / lost ⇨

_____

3 has / white fur / She / and a short tail ⇨

_____

4 my hedgehog, / am looking for / I / Spike ⇨

_____

5 lost / I / in the playground / him ⇨

_____

6 has / tiny eyes / He / and sharp spines ⇨

_____

(New Words) mall 쇼핑몰 | fur 털 | tiny eyes 아주 작은 눈 | sharp spine 뾰족한 가시

B 그림을 보고, 주어진 단어를 이용해 문장을 써 보세요.

> 나는 내 앵무새,
> 코튼(Cotton, 수컷)을 찾고 있어요.
> 나는 그것을 마당에서 잃어버렸어요.
> 그것은 아름다운 깃털과
> 긴 부리를 가지고 있어요.

_____

_____

_____

parrot 앵무새   yard 마당   feather 깃털   beak 부리

CHECK! CHECK! ☐ 첫 글자는 대문자로 썼나요? ☐ 구두점은 찍었나요? ☐ 단어와 단어 사이는 띄어 썼나요?

Unit 04 A Fun School Festival 재미있는 학교 축제(SNS)

 151

Read to Write

1 **The school festival will start** on Wednesday at 3:00 p.m. 학교 축제가 수요일 오후 3시에 시작할 거예요.　　[주제]

2 **Please visit** the main hall. 중앙홀을 방문해 보세요.　　[세부사항 1]

3 **There will be** a concert. 콘서트가 있을 거예요.　　[세부사항 2]

Step 0　패턴 이해하기

1 어떤 행사가
무슨 요일 몇 시에 있나요?
⇒ **The school festival will start** + on Wednesday at 3:00 p.m.
on Wednesday(수요일에)처럼 요일 앞에는 전치사 on을 써요. will은 '~일 것이다'라는 의미로, 미래의 일을 나타낼 때 쓰는 조동사예요.

2 어디로 가야 하나요?
⇒ **Please visit** + the main hall.
visit은 '~을 방문하다'라는 의미로, 뒤에 장소를 나타내는 말을 쓰면 돼요. please를 붙이면 좀 더 공손한 표현이 돼요.

3 어떤 행사가 있나요?
⇒ **There will be** + a concert.
There will be ~는 '~이 있을 거다'라는 의미예요. There is[are] ~는 '~이 있다'라는 뜻인데, will과 함께 쓰여 미래를 나타내고 있어요.

Step 1　표현 파악하기　듣고, 따라 말해 보세요.

 152

1
the science festival
과학 축제
⇩

2
the science classroom
과학 교실
⇩

3
a poster presentation 포스터 발표
*연구 내용을 여러 패널에 부착, 게시하여 연구를 발표하는 방법

4
the talent show
장기자랑
⇩

5
the auditorium
강당
⇩

6
many performances
많은 공연

A 듣고, 따라 말한 후 완전한 문장을 써 보세요.

153

1

| The science festival will start | + | on Thursday at 2:00 p.m. |

2

| Please visit | + | the science classroom. |

3

| There will be | + | a poster presentation. |

4

| The talent show will start | + | on Friday at 3:00 p.m. |

5

| Please visit | + | the auditorium. |

6

| There will be | + | many performances. |

154

B 듣고, 문장의 빈칸을 채운 후 전체 문장을 다시 써 보세요.

1 The science festival will start ____ Thursday at 2:00 p.m. ⇨

2 The talent show will start ____ Friday ____ 3:00 p.m. ⇨

3 _____ the science classroom. ⇨

4 Please _____ . ⇨

5 _____ a poster presentation. ⇨

6 There ____ performances. ⇨

A 주어진 말을 바르게 배열해 문장을 완성하세요. 듣고, 문장 확인 후 뜻을 써 보세요.

1 will start / on Saturday / at 10:00 a.m. / ⇨

The sports event

_____

2 visit / the gym / Please ⇨

_____

3 There / a running race / will be ⇨

_____

4 The cooking show / at 11:00 a.m. / ⇨

will start / on Wednesday

_____

5 the cooking room / Please / visit ⇨

_____

6 There / a cooking competition after / ⇨

will be

_____

New Words event 행사 I gym 체육관 I running race 달리기 경주 I cooking show 요리 쇼 I competition 대회
after 후에, 나중에

B 그림을 보고, 주어진 단어를 이용해 문장을 써 보세요.

미술 전시회가 일요일 오전 11시에 시작할 거예요. 미술실을 방문해 보세요. 학생들의 그림 전시품들이 있을 거예요.

_____

_____

_____

art exhibition 미술 전시회   art room 미술실   exhibit 전시품   drawing 그림

CHECK!
CHECK! ☐ 첫 글자는 대문자로 썼나요?   ☐ 구두점은 찍었나요?   ☐ 단어와 단어 사이는 띄어 썼나요?

A 우리말에 맞게 빈칸에 알맞은 단어를 골라 써 보세요.

1 나는 공원에서 강아지를 잃어버렸어요. 그것은 털이 검은색이에요.

I lost my dog in the _____. She has _____ fur.

bus stop / park   blue / black

2 중앙홀을 방문해 보세요. 콘서트가 있을 거예요.

Please _____ the main hall. There will be a _____.

show / visit   presentation / concert

3 이번 주 화요일에 뭐 할 거야? 같이 경기장에 가자.

What are you doing this _____? Let's go to the _____.

Tuesday / Wednesday   beach / stadium

B 질문에 알맞은 답을 <보기>에서 골라 써 보세요.

1 What can we do together? ⇨

우리는 무엇을 함께 할 수 있나요?

2 What can you do in the river? ⇨

당신은 강에서 무엇을 할 수 있나요?

3 What are you looking for? ⇨

당신은 무엇을 찾고 있나요?

4 What does she look like? ⇨

그녀는 어떻게 생겼나요?

5 When will the school festival start? ⇨

학교 축제는 언제 시작하나요?

보기

> She has black fur.   I can fish in the river.   We can have fun together.
> The school festival will start on Wednesday at 3:00 p.m.   I am looking for my dog.

C 주어진 말을 바르게 배열해 완전한 문장을 써 보세요.

1 go to / Let's / the beach ⇨

2 really / is / The dress / awesome ⇨

3 so friendly / are / You ⇨

4 her / lost / I / at the bus stop ⇨

5 visit / the auditorium / Please ⇨

6 a running race / will / There / be ⇨

D 문장을 보고, 틀린 부분을 알맞게 고쳐 보세요.

1 The art exhibition Will starts on sunday ⇨

at 11:00 a.m. 미술 전시회가 일요일 오전 11시에 시작할 거예요.

2 i is looking For my parrot. ⇨

나는 내 앵무새를 찾고 있어요.

3 it have beautiful feathers And a long beak. ⇨

그것은 아름다운 깃털과 긴 부리가 있어요.

4 thank You for the sunglass. ⇨

선글라스 고마워.

5 what Am you doing this monday? ⇨

이번 주 월요일에 뭐 할 거야?

6 we Can sees pandas. ⇨

우리는 판다를 볼 수 있어.

Unit 05 Last Vacation 지난 방학(온라인 채팅)

Read to Write

① A: **What did you do** last winter vacation?   [주제]
지난 겨울 방학에 뭐 했어?

② B: **I went skiing** on a mountain. 산에 스키를 타러 갔어.   [세부사항 1]

③ **I learned** Chinese, too. 나는 중국어도 배웠어.   [세부사항 2]

Step 0   패턴 이해하기

① 지난 방학 때 무엇을 했나요?   ➡ **What did you do** + last winter vacation?
(질문할 때)
last는 '지난'이라는 뜻으로, What did you do last ~?는 '지난 ~에 뭐 했어?'라는 의미예요.

② (어디에) 무엇을 하러 갔나요?   ➡ **I went skiing** + on a mountain.
go skiing은 '스키 타러 가다'란 뜻인데, 여기서는 과거의 일에 대해 말하는 것이므로 go 대신에 과거형인 went를 써서 went skiing으로 썼어요.

③ 또 무엇을 했나요?   ➡ **I learned** + Chinese, too.
learn은 '배우다'라는 뜻으로, 여기서는 과거를 나타내므로 learned를 썼어요. too가 '~도, 역시'라는 뜻으로 쓰일 때는 문장 맨 뒤에 와요.

Step 1   표현 파악하기   듣고, 따라 말해 보세요.

1
last spring vacation
지난 봄 방학(에)
⇩

4
last summer vacation
지난 여름 방학(에)
⇩

2
fish on a lake
호수에서 낚시하다
⇩

5
surf at the beach
바닷가에서 서핑하다
⇩

3
visit my grandparents
조부모님을 방문하다

6
join a robot class
로봇 수업에 참가하다

A 듣고, 따라 말한 후 완전한 문장을 써 보세요.

1		What did you do	+	last spring vacation?
2		I went fishing	+	on a lake.
3		I visited	+	my grandparents, too.

4		What did you do	+	last summer vacation?
5		I went surfing	+	at the beach.
6		I joined	+	a robot class, too.

B 듣고, 문장의 빈칸을 채운 후 전체 문장을 다시 써 보세요.

1 What _____ last spring vacation? ⇨

2 What did you do _____ vacation? ⇨

3 _____ on a lake. ⇨

4 I went surfing _____ . ⇨

5 _____ my grandparents, too. ⇨

6 I _____ class, too. ⇨

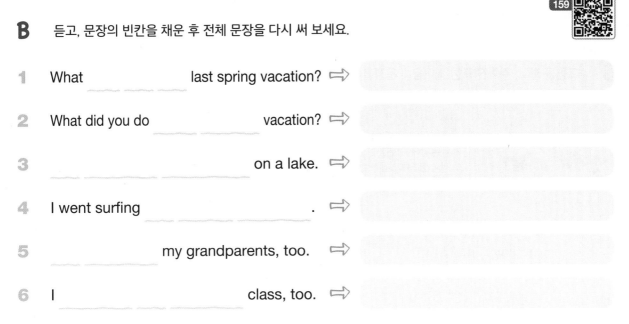

A 주어진 말을 바르게 배열해 문장을 완성하세요. 듣고, 문장 확인 후 뜻을 써 보세요.

1 did you do / last winter vacation? / What ⇨
_____

2 went bowling / I / with my friends ⇨
_____

3 visited / my uncle, / I / too ⇨
_____

4 did you do / What / last spring vacation? ⇨
_____

5 went camping / with my family / I ⇨
_____

6 to / learned / I / dance, / too ⇨
_____

New Words go bowling 볼링을 치러 가다 | go camping 캠핑을 가다

B 그림을 보고, 주어진 표현을 이용해 문장을 써 보세요.

A: 지난 여름 방학에 뭐 했어?
B: 나는 강에 카약을 타러 갔어.
과학 캠프에도 참가했어.

A: _____

B: _____
_____

go kayaking 카약을 타러 가다   join a science camp 과학 캠프에 참가하다

CHECK!
CHECK!   ☐ 첫 글자는 대문자로 썼나요?   ☐ 구두점은 찍었나요?   ☐ 단어와 단어 사이는 띄어 썼나요?

Finding Lost Items 분실물 찾아주기(온라인 채팅)

161

Read to Write

❶ A: **I found** these glasses in the classroom.   [주제]
이 안경을 교실에서 발견했어.

❷ **Whose glasses** are they? 누구 안경이지?   [세부사항 1]

(A가 보내 준 사진을 보고)

❸ B: **I think** that they are Emma's. 그거 엠마 거 같아.   [세부사항 2]

Step 0   패턴 이해하기

❶ 어디에서 발견했나요?   ⇒ **I found** + these glasses in the classroom.

found는 find의 과거형으로, 'I found + 물건 + in + 장소'는 '나는 ~에서 …을 발견했다'란 의미예요.

❷ 물건의 주인을 물을 때는?   ⇒ **Whose glasses** + are they?

whose는 '누구의'라는 뜻으로, Whose glasses는 '누구의 안경'이라는 의미예요.

❸ 누구의 것일까요?   ⇒ **I think** + that they are Emma's.

'I think that + 주어 + 동사'는 '나는 ~라고 생각한다'라는 의미예요. '~의 것'이라고 소유를 나타낼 때는 '이름 + 's'로 써요. 원래는 Emma's glasses인데 앞에 나온 것과 중복을 피하기 위해서 glasses가 생략된 거예요.

Step 1   표현 파악하기   듣고, 따라 말해 보세요.

162

1
in the playground
운동장에서
⇩

4
in the music room
음악실에서
⇩

2
cell phone
휴대전화
⇩

5
bag
가방
⇩

3
Olivia's
올리비아의 (것)

6
Emily's
에밀리의 (것)

A   듣고, 따라 말한 후 완전한 문장을 써 보세요.

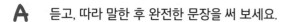

1		I found	+	this in the playground.
2		Whose cell phone	+	is it?
3		I think	+	that it's Olivia's.

4		I found	+	this in the music room.
5		Whose bag	+	is it?
6		I think	+	that it's Emily's.

B   듣고, 문장의 빈칸을 채운 후 전체 문장을 다시 써 보세요.

1 _____ in the playground. ⇨

2 I _____ the music room. ⇨

3 _____ it? ⇨

4 _____ ? ⇨

5 _____ it's Olivia's. ⇨

6 I _____ that _____ . ⇨

A   주어진 말을 바르게 배열해 문장을 완성하세요. 듣고, 문장 확인 후 뜻을 써 보세요.

1   found / I / in the gym / these   ⇨

2   are / Whose shoes / they?   ⇨

3   think / they are Amella's / I / that   ⇨

4   found / I / in the art room / this   ⇨

5   Whose bottle / it? / is   ⇨

6   that / think / I / it's Milo's.   ⇨

New Words   bottle 병

B   그림을 보고, 주어진 단어를 이용해 문장을 써 보세요.

A: 나 이거 과학 실험실에서 발견했어.
이거 누구 공책이야?
B: 그거 데이브(Dave) 거 같아.

A:

B:

science lab 과학 실험실   notebook 공책

CHECK!
CHECK!   ☐ 첫 글자는 대문자로 썼나요?   ☐ 구두점은 찍었나요?   ☐ 단어와 단어 사이는 띄어 썼나요?

Unit 07 My Dream Job 나의 장래 희망(블로그)

Read to Write

1 **I want to be** a cartoonist. 나는 만화가가 되고 싶어요. [주제]

2 **I like to** draw cartoons. 나는 만화 그리는 것을 좋아해요. [세부사항 1]

3 **Creating a cartoon character is like** magic. [세부사항 2]
만화 캐릭터를 만드는 것은 마치 마술 같아요.

Step 0 패턴 이해하기

1 무엇이 되고 싶나요?
⇨ **I want to be** + a cartoonist.
'I want to be + 직업명'은 '나는 ~이 되고 싶어요'라는 뜻으로, 장래 희망을 나타낼 때 쓸 수 있어요.

2 무슨 일을 좋아하나요?
⇨ **I like to** + draw cartoons.
I like to ~는 '나는 ~하는 것을 좋아한다'라는 의미로, to 다음에는 동사원형이 와요.

3 그 일을 비유하자면?
⇨ **Creating a cartoon character is like** + magic.
여기서 like는 '~ 같은'이라는 뜻으로, 뒤에 명사가 와요.

Step 1 표현 파악하기 듣고, 따라 말해 보세요.

1
a soccer player
축구 선수
⇩
2
play soccer
축구를 하다
⇩
3
an adventure
모험

4
a chef
요리사
⇩
5
cook new food
새로운 음식을 만들다
⇩
6
magic
마법

A 듣고, 따라 말한 후 완전한 문장을 써 보세요.

1   I want to be   +   a soccer player.

2   I like to   +   play soccer.

3   Playing soccer is like   +   an adventure.

4   I want to be   +   a chef.

5   I like to   +   cook new food.

6   Cooking is like   +   magic.

B 듣고, 문장의 빈칸을 채운 후 전체 문장을 다시 써 보세요.

1   _____ be a soccer player.   ⇨

2   I want _____ .   ⇨

3   _____ play soccer.   ⇨

4   I like _____ .   ⇨

5   _____ is like an adventure.   ⇨

6   _____ magic.   ⇨

패턴 문장 만들기

170

A 주어진 말을 바르게 배열해 문장을 완성하세요. 듣고, 문장 확인 후 뜻을 써 보세요.

1 want / to be / a dancer / I ⇨

2 like / I / to dance ⇨

3 like a movie / Dancing / is ⇨

4 want / to be / I / a singer ⇨

5 like / I / to sing songs ⇨

6 Singing / like a story / is ⇨

New Words dancer 댄서

B 그림을 보고, 주어진 단어를 이용해 문장을 써 보세요.

나는 경찰관이 되고 싶어요.
나는 사람들을 돕는 것을 좋아해요.
사람을 돕는 것은
영웅이 되는 것 같아요.

police officer 경찰관   help 돕다   hero 영웅

CHECK!
CHECK!   ☐ 첫 글자는 대문자로 썼나요?   ☐ 구두점은 찍었나요?   ☐ 단어와 단어 사이는 띄어 썼나요?

171

Read to Write

① **I want Lego** for my Christmas gift.   [주제]
나는 크리스마스 선물로 레고를 받고 싶어요.

② **I can make** anything with it.   [세부사항 1]
나는 그것으로 뭐든 만들 수 있어요.

③ **Lego is** fun. 레고는 재밌어요.   [세부사항 2]

Step 0 **패턴 이해하기**

① 무엇을 받고 싶나요?   ⇒ **I want Lego** + for my Christmas gift.
I want ~는 '나는 ~을 원한다'란 뜻이에요. for는 '~로'라는 의미로, for my Christmas gift는 '크리스마스 선물로'라는 뜻이에요.

② 그걸로 무엇을 할 수 있나요?   ⇒ **I can make** + anything with it.
'I can + 동사원형'은 '나는 ~할 수 있다'란 의미로, can이 조동사여서 뒤에 동사원형인 make가 왔어요. anything은 '무엇이든'이라는 의미예요.

③ 그것은 어떤가요?   ⇒ **Lego is** + fun.
fun은 명사로 '재미', 형용사로 '재미있는'이란 뜻이에요.

172

Step 1 **표현 파악하기** 듣고, 따라 말해 보세요.

1
a skateboard
스케이트보드
⇩

2
ride
(차량·자전거 등을) 타다
⇩

3
fast
빠른

4
clay
점토
⇩

5
get rid of stress
스트레스를 없애다
⇩

6
soft
부드러운

A 듣고, 따라 말한 후 완전한 문장을 써 보세요.

1		I want a skateboard	+	for my birthday gift.
2		I can ride it	+	in the park.
3		A skateboard is	+	fast.

4		I want clay	+	for my Children's Day gift.
5		I can get rid of	+	stress.
6		Clay is	+	soft.

B 듣고, 문장의 빈칸을 채운 후 전체 문장을 다시 써 보세요.

1 _____ a skateboard for my birthday gift. ⇨

2 I want _____ Children's Day gift. ⇨

3 _____ it in the park. ⇨

4 I can _____ stress. ⇨

5 _____ fast. ⇨

6 _____ . ⇨

A 주어진 말을 바르게 배열해 문장을 완성하세요. 듣고, 문장 확인 후 뜻을 써 보세요.

1 want / for my / Christmas gift / I / chocolate / ⇨ _____

2 I / feel happy / can ⇨ _____

3 is / delicious / Chocolate ⇨ _____

4 want / I / for my New Year's Day gift / ⇨ new shoes _____

5 I / run faster / can ⇨ _____

6 are / New shoes / necessary ⇨ _____

(New Words) run faster 더 빨리 달리다 | necessary 필요한

B 그림을 보고, 주어진 단어를 이용해 문장을 써 보세요.

나는 크리스마스 선물로
요리책을 받고 싶어요.
나는 그것으로 무엇이든
요리할 수 있어요.
요리책은 도움이 돼요.

_____

_____

_____

cookbook 요리책   **anything** 무엇이든   **helpful** 도움이 되는

CHECK! CHECK! ☐ 첫 글자는 대문자로 썼나요?   ☐ 구두점은 찍었나요?   ☐ 단어와 단어 사이는 띄어 썼나요?

A 우리말에 맞게 빈칸에 알맞은 단어를 골라 써 보세요.

1 A: 이것은 누구의 안경인가요?   B: 그거 엠마 거 같아요.

A: Whose _____ are these?   B: I think that they are _____.

glasses / socks   Olivia's / Emma's

2 나는 새로운 요리를 하는 것을 좋아해요. 요리는 마법 같아요.

I like to _____. Cooking is like _____.

cook new food / play soccer   adventure / magic

3 나는 크리스마스 선물로 레고를 받고 싶어요. 레고는 재밌어요.

I want Lego for my _____ gift. Lego is _____.

birthday / Christmas   fast / fun

B 질문에 알맞은 답을 <보기>에서 골라 써 보세요.

1 What did you do last winter vacation? ⇨

당신은 지난 겨울 방학에 뭐 했어요?

2 Where did you find them?   ⇨

당신은 그것을 어디에서 발견했어요?

3 What do you want to be?   ⇨

당신은 무엇이 되고 싶어요?

4 What can we do?   ⇨

우리는 무엇을 할 수 있나요?

5 What else did you do?   ⇨

당신은 또 무엇을 했나요?

보기

I want to be a cartoonist.   I learned Chinese, too.   We can read new books.
I went skiing on a mountain.   I found these glasses in the classroom.

C 주어진 말을 바르게 배열해 완전한 문장을 써 보세요.

1 cell phone / Whose / this? / is ⇨

2 went / in the river / I / kayaking ⇨

3 visited / too / my uncle, / I ⇨

4 is / an adventure / like / Playing soccer ⇨

5 in the park / can / I / it / ride ⇨

6 is / A cookbook / helpful ⇨

D 문장을 보고, 틀린 부분을 알맞게 고쳐 보세요.

1 i wants clay For my children's Day gift. ⇨

나는 어린이날 선물로 점토를 받고 싶어요.

2 helping people are like be a hero. ⇨

사람을 돕는 것은 영웅이 되는 것 같아요.

3 a skateboard are Fast. ⇨

스케이트보드는 빨라요.

4 i likes To dance. ⇨

나는 춤추는 것을 좋아해요.

5 i Found this In the science lab. ⇨

나 이거 과학 실험실에서 발견했어요.

6 I Think that Its Dave's. ⇨

그거 데이브 거 같아.

Read to Write

176

① **I have** a cold. 나는 감기에 걸렸어요.　　　　　　　　[주제]

② **I didn't go** to school today.　　　　　　　　　　　　[세부사항 1]
나는 오늘 학교에 가지 않았어요.

③ **I went to** the doctor. 나는 병원에 갔어요.　　　　　　[세부사항 2]

Step 0 패턴 이해하기

① 어디가 아픈가요?　　⇨ **I have** + a cold.
'I have + 질병명'은 '~가 아프다, ~에 걸리다'라는 의미예요.

② 무엇을 안 했나요?　　⇨ **I didn't go** + to school today.
'I didn't + 동사원형'은 '나는 ~하지 않았다'란 의미예요. 과거의 일이기 때문에
don't의 과거형인 didn't를 썼어요.

③ 무엇을 했나요?　　⇨ **I went to** + the doctor.
go to the doctor는 '병원에 가다'라는 의미예요. 마찬가지로 과거의 일이기 때문
에 go의 과거형인 went를 썼어요.

Step 1 표현 파악하기　　듣고, 따라 말해 보세요.

177

1
have a headache
머리가 아프다
⇩

4
have a toothache
이가 아프다
⇩

2
do my homework
숙제를 하다
⇩

5
eat lunch
점심을 먹다
⇩

3
go to bed early
일찍 자다

6
go to the dentist
치과에 가다

A 듣고, 따라 말한 후 완전한 문장을 써 보세요.

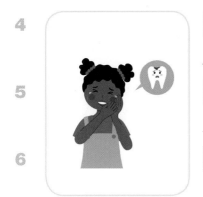

1	I have	+	a headache.
2	I didn't do	+	my homework today.
3	I went to	+	bed early.
4	I have	+	a toothache.
5	I didn't eat	+	lunch today.
6	I went to	+	the dentist.

B 듣고, 문장의 빈칸을 채운 후 전체 문장을 다시 써 보세요.

1 I _____ . ⇨

2 _____ . ⇨

3 _____ do my homework today. ⇨

4 I _____ . ⇨

5 I _____ early. ⇨

6 I _____ . ⇨

Step 3 패턴 문장 만들기

A 주어진 말을 바르게 배열해 문장을 완성하세요. 듣고, 문장 확인 후 뜻을 써 보세요.

1   a backache / have / I   ⇨ _____

2   didn't take / I / P.E. class / today   ⇨ _____

3   went to / the nurse's office / I   ⇨ _____

4   have / I / a sore throat   ⇨ _____

5   didn't / I / a word / today / say   ⇨ _____

6   went to / the doctor / I   ⇨ _____

(New Words) have a backache 허리가 아프다 I nurse's office 보건실 I have a sore throat 목이 아프다

B 그림을 보고, 주어진 표현을 이용해 문장을 써 보세요.

발진이 났어요.
나는 오늘 친구를 안 만났어요.
나는 그녀와 전화를 했어요.

_____

have a rash 발진이 나다   **talk on the phone** 전화하다, 통화하다

CHECK!
CHECK! ☐ 첫 글자는 대문자로 썼나요? ☐ 구두점은 찍었나요? ☐ 단어와 단어 사이는 띄어 썼나요?

Read to Write

1 **Let me tell you** about my morning.　　[주제]
나의 아침에 대해 말해 줄게요.

2 **I get up** at 7 o'clock. 나는 7시에 일어나요.　　[세부사항 1]

3 **I go to school** at 8 o'clock.　　[세부사항 2]
나는 8시에 학교에 가요.

Step 0　**패턴 이해하기**

1 하루의 어느 때에 대해 말하나요?　⇨　**Let me tell you** + about my morning.
'Let me + 동사원형'은 '내가 ~할게요'라는 뜻으로, Let me tell you about ~은 '내가 ~에 대해 말해 줄게요'라는 의미가 돼요.

2 몇 시에 무엇을 하나요?　⇨　**I get up** + at 7 o'clock.
get up은 '일어나다'라는 의미예요. 몇 시에 하는지 말할 때는 'at + 시각'을 쓰는데, 정각일 경우 뒤에 o'clock을 붙여 at 7 o'clock(7시에)처럼 말해요.

3 또 무엇을 하나요?　⇨　**I go to school** + at 8 o'clock.
go to school은 '학교에 가다', at 8 o'clock은 '8시에'라는 의미예요.

Step 1　**표현 파악하기**　듣고, 따라 말해 보세요.

1
my afternoon
나의 오후
⇩

2
have lunch
점심을 먹다
⇩

3
play with my friend
친구와 놀다

4
my evening
나의 저녁
⇩

5
have dinner
저녁을 먹다
⇩

6
walk my dog
개를 산책시키다

A 듣고, 따라 말한 후 완전한 문장을 써 보세요.

1	Let me tell you	+	about my afternoon.
2	I have lunch	+	at 12 o'clock.
3	I play with my friend	+	after school.

4	Let me tell you	+	about my evening.
5	I have dinner	+	at 7 o'clock.
6	I walk my dog	+	after dinner.

B 듣고, 문장의 빈칸을 채운 후 전체 문장을 다시 써 보세요.

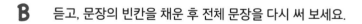

1 _____ you about my afternoon. ⇨

2 Let _____ about my evening. ⇨

3 _____ at 12 o'clock. ⇨

4 I _____ 7 o'clock. ⇨

5 _____ my friend after school. ⇨

6 I _____ after dinner. ⇨

A 주어진 말을 바르게 배열해 문장을 완성하세요. 듣고, 문장 확인 후 뜻을 써 보세요.

1 you / about my Sunday / Let me tell ⇨

_____

2 get up late / at about 9 a.m. / I ⇨

_____

3 have brunch / I / with my family ⇨

_____

4 you / Let me tell / about my Saturday ⇨

_____

5 jog / I / at 7 o'clock / around the park ⇨

_____

6 I / all day / read a book ⇨

_____

New Words   get up late 늦게 일어나다 | about ~쯤, ~경 | have brunch 브런치(아침 겸 점심)를 먹다 | all day 온종일

B 그림을 보고, 주어진 표현을 이용해 문장을 써 보세요.

나의 일요일에 대해 말해 줄게.
나는 오후 3시쯤에 영화를 봐.
나는 팝콘을 먹고 콜라를 마셔.

_____

_____

watch a movie 영화를 보다   eat popcorn 팝콘을 먹다   drink cola 콜라를 마시다

CHECK! CHECK! ☐ 첫 글자는 대문자로 썼나요?   ☐ 구두점은 찍었나요?   ☐ 단어와 단어 사이는 띄어 썼나요?

Unit 11 Safety Rules 안전 규칙(홈페이지)

 186

Read to Write

① **Here are** the school rules. 여기 학교 규칙들이 있어요. [주제]

② **Be nice** to other people. 다른 사람들에게 친절하세요. [세부사항 1]

③ **Don't run** in the hallways. 복도에서 뛰지 마세요. [세부사항 2]

Step 0 패턴 이해하기

① 어디에서 지켜야 할 규칙인가요? ⇨ **Here are** + the school rules.

Here are[is] ~는 '여기 ~이 있다'라는 의미예요. 뒤에 나오는 명사가 여러 개일 때는 Here are ~를, 한 개일 때는 Here is ~를 써요.

② 첫 번째 규칙은 무엇인가요? ⇨ **Be nice** + to other people.

'~하세요'라는 명령문은 동사원형으로 시작해요. Be nice는 '친절히 하세요', to other people은 '다른 사람들에게'라는 의미예요.

③ 두 번째 규칙은 무엇인가요? ⇨ **Don't run** + in the hallways.

'~하지 마세요'라는 부정 명령문은 동사원형 앞에 Don't를 붙여 줘요. 여기서는 run 앞에 Don't를 붙여 '뛰지 마세요'란 뜻의 부정 명령문이 되었어요.

Step 1 표현 파악하기 듣고, 따라 말해 보세요.

 187

1
the museum rules
박물관 규칙들
⇩

2
be quiet around the exhibits
전시품 주변에서 조용히 하다
⇩

3
eat
먹다

4
the zoo rules
동물원 규칙들
⇩

5
be careful near the pond
연못 근처에서 조심하다
⇩

6
feed the animals
동물에게 먹이를 주다

A 듣고, 따라 말한 후 완전한 문장을 써 보세요.

1 Here are   +   the museum rules.

2 Be quiet   +   around the exhibits.

3 Don't eat   +   in the museum.

4 Here are   +   the zoo rules.

5 Be careful   +   near the pond.

6 Don't feed   +   the animals.

B 듣고, 문장의 빈칸을 채운 후 전체 문장을 다시 써 보세요.

1 _____ rules. ⇨

2 Here _____ . ⇨

3 _____ the exhibits. ⇨

4 Be _____ . ⇨

5 _____ the museum. ⇨

6 _____ . ⇨

A 주어진 말을 바르게 배열해 문장을 완성하세요. 듣고, 문장 확인 후 뜻을 써 보세요.

190

1 the bus rules / are / Here ⇨

2 in / your seat / Stay ⇨

3 shout / Don't ⇨

4 are / Here / the library rules ⇨

5 quiet, / please / Be ⇨

6 the books / draw / Don't / in ⇨

(New Words) stay 머무르다 | seat 자리 | shout 소리를 지르다 | draw 그림을 그리다

B 그림을 보고, 주어진 단어를 이용해 문장을 써 보세요.

여기 수영장 규칙들이 있어요.
수영모를 써 주세요.
수영장에 쓰레기를
버리지 마세요.

pool rules 수영장 규칙 **swimming cap** 수영모자 **litter** 쓰레기를 버리다 **swimming pool** 수영장

CHECK!
CHECK!   ☐ 첫 글자는 대문자로 썼나요?   ☐ 구두점은 찍었나요?   ☐ 단어와 단어 사이는 띄어 썼나요?

Unit 12 Flea Market Advertisements
벼룩시장 광고(홈페이지)

191

Read to Write

① **These gloves are** so pretty. 이 장갑은 아주 예뻐요. [주제]

② **They are only** two **dollars.** 이건 단 2달러예요. [세부사항 1]

③ **You can wear the gloves** on cold days. [세부사항 2]
당신은 추운 날에 장갑을 낄 수 있어요.

Step 0 패턴 이해하기

① 무슨 물건인가요? ⇨ **These gloves are** + so pretty.
These gloves는 '이 장갑'이라는 의미예요. 가까이 있는 여러 개를 가리킬 때는 these를 쓰고, 멀리 있는 여러 개를 가리킬 때는 those를 써요.

② 그것은 얼마인가요? ⇨ **They are** + **only** two **dollars.**
They are ~ dollars는 '그것들은 ~달러이다'라는 의미예요. only는 '(수나 양이) 단지 ~밖에'라는 의미로 쓰였어요.

③ 무엇을 할 수 있나요? ⇨ **You can wear the gloves** + on cold days.
can은 '~할 수 있다'라는 의미로 뒤에 동사원형이 와요. on cold days는 '추운 날에'라는 의미예요.

Step 1 표현 파악하기 듣고, 따라 말해 보세요.

192

1
these boots / cute
이 부츠 / 귀여운
⇩

4
these jeans / fashionable
이 청바지 / 유행하는
⇩

2
five dollars
5달러
⇩

5
six dollars
6달러
⇩

3
the boots / in winter
부츠 / 겨울에

6
the jeans / to a party
청바지 / 파티에

A   듣고, 따라 말한 후 완전한 문장을 써 보세요.

1   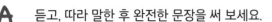   These boots are   +   so cute.

2   They are   +   only five dollars.

3   You can wear the boots   +   in winter.

4   These jeans are   +   so fashionable.

5   They are   +   only six dollars.

6   You can wear the jeans   +   to a party.

B   듣고, 문장의 빈칸을 채운 후 전체 문장을 다시 써 보세요.

1   _____ so cute.   ⇨

2   These _____ fashionable.   ⇨

3   _____ five dollars.   ⇨

4   They _____ dollars.   ⇨

5   _____ the boots in winter.   ⇨

6   You _____ the jeans to a party.   ⇨

Step 3 패턴 문장 만들기

A 주어진 말을 바르게 배열해 문장을 완성하세요. 듣고, 문장 확인 후 뜻을 써 보세요.

1 are / so stylish / These shorts ⇨ _____

_____

2 are / only two dollars / They ⇨ _____

_____

3 wear the shorts / can / in summer / You ⇨ _____

_____

4 are / These shoes / so comfortable ⇨ _____

_____

5 They / only four dollars / are ⇨ _____

_____

6 walk a lot with them / can / You / ⇨ _____

in the playground

_____

(New Words) stylish 멋진 I shorts 반바지 I comfortable 편안한 I a lot 많이

B 그림을 보고, 주어진 단어를 이용해 문장을 써 보세요.

이 샌들은 정말 최신 유행이에요.
이건 단지 5 달러예요.
당신은 밖에서 샌들을
신을 수 있어요.

_____

_____

_____

sandals 샌달   **trendy** 최신 유행하는   **outside** 밖에서

CHECK!
CHECK! ☐ 첫 글자는 대문자로 썼나요? ☐ 구두점은 찍었나요? ☐ 단어와 단어 사이는 띄어 썼나요?

A 우리말에 맞게 빈칸에 알맞은 단어를 골라 써 보세요.

1 나의 아침에 대해 말해 줄게요. 나는 8시에 일어나요.

Let me tell you about my _____. I _____ at 8 o'clock.

morning / evening   get up / go to school

2 다른 사람들에게 친절하세요. 복도에서 뛰지 마세요.

Be _____ to other people. Don't _____ in the hallways.

nice / careful   feed / run

3 이 장갑은 아주 예뻐요. 당신은 추운 날에 장갑을 낄 수 있어요.

These gloves are so _____. You can _____ the gloves on cold days.

comfortable / pretty   wear / buy

B 질문에 알맞은 답을 <보기>에서 골라 써 보세요.

1 Are you sick? What's the matter? ⇨

아파요? 뭐가 문제인가요?

2 What time do you have dinner? ⇨

당신은 몇 시에 저녁을 먹나요?

3 What is one of the museum rules? ⇨

박물관 규칙 중 하나는 무엇인가요?

4 How much are they? ⇨

그것들은 얼마인가요?

5 When do you walk your dog? ⇨

당신은 언제 개를 산책시키나요?

보기

Don't eat in the museum.   I walk my dog after dinner.

I have dinner at 7 o'clock.   I have a cold.   They are only two dollars.

C 주어진 말을 바르게 배열해 완전한 문장을 써 보세요.

1 are / so stylish / These shorts ⇨

2 are / They / only four dollars ⇨

3 feed / Don't / the animals ⇨

4 watch a movie / at about 3 p.m. / I ⇨

5 me / tell / Let / you / about my Saturday ⇨

6 have / I / a backache ⇨

D 문장을 보고, **틀린** 부분을 알맞게 고쳐 보세요.

1 You Can wears tHe sandals Outside. ⇨

당신은 그 샌들을 밖에서 신을 수 있어요.

2 Here is the pool Rules. ⇨

여기 수영장 규칙들이 있어요.

3 Don't draws In the Books. ⇨

책에 그림 그리지 마세요.

4 Was careful Near the pond. ⇨

연못 근처에서 조심하세요.

5 he eats popcorn and drank cola. ⇨

나는 팝콘을 먹고 콜라를 마셔요.

6 i don't says The word. ⇨

나는 한 마디도 하지 않았어요.

PART 4

순서를 나타내는 글쓰기

순서를 나타내는 글쓰기는 어떤 일을 시간이나 과정의 순서대로 나타내는 글쓰기입니다. 이런 글은 다른 사람들에게 어떤 일이 어떻게 이뤄지는지 이해시키기 위한 좋은 방법이에요.

<순서를 나타내는 글쓰기 방법>

1. 주제를 정하면 일들을 순서대로 나열합니다. 시간이나 사건의 순서대로 처음부터 끝까지 그 과정을 명확하게 설명하세요.
2. 순서를 나타내는 단어나 구문을 사용하여 명확하게 표현하세요. 예를 들어, first(처음에), next(다음에), then(다음에), finally(마지막으로) 등을 사용할 수 있어요.

예를 들어, 내가 아침에 일어나서 하는 일에 대해 쓴다면 다음과 같이 할 수 있습니다. 무엇을 써야 할지 잘 모르겠다면 질문에 대한 답을 적어 나간다고 생각해 보세요. 답을 적어 나가다 보면 어느새 내가 아침에 일어나 하는 일에 대한 순서를 나타내는 글이 완성됩니다.

예시

첫 번째 하는 일	아침에 가장 먼저 하는 일은 무엇인가요?	**First, I wake up in the morning.**
두 번째 하는 일	그 다음에 하는 일은 무엇인가요?	**Second, I brush my teeth and wash my face.**
세 번째 하는 일	마지막에 하는 일은 무엇인가요?	**Last, I get dressed and have breakfast.**

Doing House Chores 집안일하기

Read to Write **How to Clean My Room** 내 방 청소하는 법   196

1 **First,** put your clothes away. 맨 먼저, 옷을 치워요.   [순서 1]

2 **Second,** make the bed. 두 번째로 침대를 정리해요.   [순서 2]

3 **Last,** vacuum the floor.   [순서 3]
마지막으로 바닥을 청소기로 청소해요.

Step 0 패턴 이해하기

1 맨 먼저 무엇을 하나요?   ⇨ **First,** + put your clothes away.

First는 '맨 먼저'라는 의미예요. put away는 '치우다'라는 뜻인데요, 이렇게 동사로 시작하는 문장을 '명령문'이라고 해요.

2 그 다음은 무엇을 하나요?   ⇨ **Second,** + make the bed.

Second은 '두 번째로', make the bed는 '침대를 정리하다'란 의미예요.

3 마지막으로는 무엇을 하나요?   ⇨ **Last,** + vacuum the floor.

Last는 '마지막으로', vacuum은 '진공 청소기로 청소하다'란 의미예요.

Step 1 표현 파악하기   듣고, 따라 말해 보세요.   197

1
plug the power cord into an outlet
전원 코드를 콘센트에 꽂다
⇩

2
switch on the power
전원을 켜다
⇩

3
push the vacuum gently
진공 청소기를 부드럽게 밀다

4
dust the furniture
가구의 먼지를 털다
⇩

5
vacuum the carpet
카펫을 진공 청소기로 청소하다
⇩

6
arrange the cushions neatly
쿠션들을 가지런히 정리하다

A 듣고, 따라 말한 후 완전한 문장을 써 보세요.

How to use a vacuum cleaner 진공청소기 사용하는 법

1	First,	+	plug the power cord into an outlet.
2	Second,	+	switch on the power.
3	Last,	+	push the vacuum gently.

How to clean the living room 거실 청소하는 법

4	First,	+	dust the furniture.
5	Second,	+	vacuum the carpet.
6	Last,	+	arrange the cushions neatly.

199

B 듣고, 문장의 빈칸을 채운 후 전체 문장을 다시 써 보세요.

1 _____, _____ the power cord into an outlet. ⇨

2 First, _____. ⇨

3 _____, _____ on the power. ⇨

4 Second, _____. ⇨

5 _____, _____ the vacuum gently. ⇨

6 _____, _____ the cushions neatly. ⇨

A 주어진 말을 바르게 배열해 문장을 완성하세요. 듣고, 문장 확인 후 뜻을 써 보세요.

How to water the plants 식물에 물 주는 법

1 fill / the watering can / First, ⇨

2 go to / Second, / the flower beds ⇨

3 the flowers / water / Last, ⇨

How to recycle 재활용하는 법

4 the paper, plastic, and glass / collect / First, ⇨

5 sort / them into bins / Second, ⇨

6 them / take / to a recycling center / Last, ⇨

(New Words) watering can 물뿌리개 | flower bed 화단 | water 물을 주다 | collect 모으다 | sort 분류하다 | bin 쓰레기통

B 그림을 보고, 주어진 단어와 표현을 이용해 문장을 써 보세요.

먼저, 쇼핑 목록을 만들어요.
두 번째로 상점에 가서
장바구니를 가져와요.
마지막으로, 식료품을
장바구니에 담아요.

How to do the grocery shopping 장보는 법

make a shopping list 쇼핑 목록을 만들다   pick up a shopping basket 장바구니를 집다
place 놓다, 두다   groceries 식료품류

CHECK! CHECK!   ☐ 첫 글자는 대문자로 썼나요?   ☐ 구두점은 찍었나요?   ☐ 단어와 단어 사이는 띄어 썼나요?

201

Read to Write

1 **First,** take bus number 7. 맨 먼저, 7번 버스를 타세요. [순서 1]

2 **Next,** get off at the library. 그 다음에 도서관에서 내리세요. [순서 2]

3 **Last,** go straight to the police station. [순서 3]
마지막으로 경찰서까지 곧장 가세요.

Step 0 패턴 이해하기

1 무엇을 타나요? ⇒ **First,** + take bus number 7.
First는 '맨 먼저'라는 의미예요. 'take + 교통수단'은 '~을 타다'란 뜻으로, 어떤 교통수단을 이용하는지 나타낼 때 쓸 수 있어요.

2 어디에서 내리나요? ⇒ **Next,** + get off at the library.
Next는 '다음에'라는 의미예요. get off는 '내리다', 'at + 장소'는 '~에서'라는 의미예요.

3 어떻게 가나요? ⇒ **Last,** + go straight to the police station.
Last는 '마지막으로', go straight to는 '~로 곧장 가다'라는 의미예요.

202

Step 1 표현 파악하기 듣고, 따라 말해 보세요.

1
take the subway
지하철을 타다
⇩

2
get off
내리다
⇩

3
turn left at the corner
코너에서 왼쪽으로 돌다

4
walk straight
곧장 걸어가다
⇩

5
cross the road
길을 건너다
⇩

6
turn right at the corner
코너에서 오른쪽으로 돌다

Step 2 패턴 문장 뼈대 잡기

A 듣고, 따라 말한 후 완전한 문장을 써 보세요.

203

How to get to the bank 은행에 가는 법

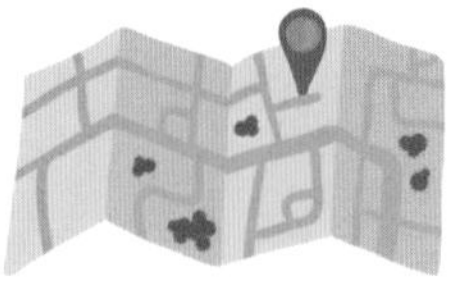

1 First, + take the subway.

2 Next, + get off at Central Station.

3 Last, + turn left at the corner.

How to get to the bakery 빵집에 가는 법

4 First, + walk straight.

5 Next, + cross the road.

6 Last, + turn right at the corner.

B 듣고, 문장의 빈칸을 채운 후 전체 문장을 다시 써 보세요.

204

1 ______ , ______ the subway. ⇨

2 First, ______ ______ . ⇨

3 ______ , ______ off at Central Station. ⇨

4 Next, ______ ______ ______ . ⇨

5 ______ , ______ left at the corner. ⇨

6 ______ , ______ ______ at the corner. ⇨

205

A 주어진 말을 바르게 배열해 문장을 완성하세요. 듣고, 문장 확인 후 뜻을 써 보세요.

How to get to the flower shop 꽃집에 가는 법

1 walk / First, / straight ⇨ ....

2 go straight / Next, / two blocks ⇨ ....

3 turn right / at the corner / Last, ⇨ ....

How to get to the bookstore 서점에 가는 법

4 take / First, / the bus ⇨ ....

5 Next, / at the mall / get off ⇨ ....

6 go down / the street / Last, ⇨ ....

(New Words) **at the mall** 쇼핑몰에서 | **go down the street** 길을 따라 가다

B 그림을 보고, 주어진 표현을 이용해 문장을 써 보세요.

먼저, 길 끝까지 걸어가세요.
그 다음에 코너에서
오른쪽으로 도세요.
마지막으로 길을 건너세요.

How to get to the school 학교 가는 법
....
....
....

walk to the end of the road 길 끝까지 걸어가다   **cross the road** 길을 건너다

CHECK!
CHECK!   ☐ 첫 글자는 대문자로 썼나요?   ☐ 구두점은 찍었나요?   ☐ 단어와 단어 사이는 띄어 썼나요?

Read to Write

1 **One day, I went to** the garden. 어느 날, 나는 정원에 갔어요.[주제]

2 **Then, I saw** some insects **there.** [세부사항 1]
그리고, 거기에서 곤충을 몇 마리 봤어요.

3 **Later, I took pictures of** butterflies. [세부사항 2]
나중에 나비들의 사진을 찍었어요.

Step 0 패턴 이해하기

1 어디에 갔나요? ⇨ **One day, + I went to +** the garden.
one day는 '어느 날'이라는 의미로, 미래와 과거 둘 다에 쓸 수 있어요. went는 go(가다)의 과거형으로, 'I went to + 장소'는 '나는 ~에 갔다'란 의미예요.

2 거기에서 무엇을 봤나요? ⇨ **Then, + I saw +** some insects **+ there.**
Then은 '그 다음에, 그리고'라는 의미예요. saw는 see(보다)의 과거형으로, I saw ~는 '~을 보았다'라는 의미예요.

3 무엇을 사진 찍었나요? ⇨ **Later, + I took pictures of +** butterflies.
Later는 '나중에'라는 의미예요. take a picture of는 '~의 사진을 찍다'란 표현인데, 여기서는 과거의 일이라서 take의 과거인 took를 썼어요.

Step 1 표현 파악하기 듣고, 따라 말해 보세요.

1 the zoo
동물원

2 some animals
동물들

3 penguins
펭귄들

4 a city
도시

5 some buildings
건물들

6 skyscrapers
고층빌딩들

A 듣고, 따라 말한 후 완전한 문장을 써 보세요.

1 | One day, | + | I went to + the zoo.

2 | Then, | + | I saw + some animals + there.

3 | Later, | + | I took pictures of + penguins.

4 | One day, | + | I went to + a city.

5 | Then, | + | I saw + some buildings + there.

6 | Later, | + | I took pictures of + skyscrapers.

B 듣고, 문장의 빈칸을 채운 후 전체 문장을 다시 써 보세요.

1 _____ , I _____ to the zoo. ⇨

2 One day, _____ a city. ⇨

3 _____ , _____ some animals there. ⇨

4 Then, I _____ buildings ____ . ⇨

5 _____ , _____ pictures of penguins. ⇨

6 Later, I _____ of skyscrapers. ⇨

Step 3   패턴 문장 만들기

A   주어진 말을 바르게 배열해 문장을 완성하세요. 듣고, 문장 확인 후 뜻을 써 보세요.

1   I / One day, / the country / went to ⇨

_____

2   I / Then, / some farm animals /
saw / there ⇨

_____

3   Later, / took pictures of / I / cows ⇨

_____

4   went to / I / the sea / One day, ⇨

_____

5   I / Then, / some sea animals /
there / saw ⇨

_____

6   dolphins / Later, / took pictures of / I ⇨

_____

(New Words)   country 시골 | farm animal 농장 동물 | sea animal 바다 동물 | dolphin 돌고래

B   그림을 보고, 주어진 단어를 이용해 문장을 써 보세요.

> 어느 날, 나는 산에 갔어요.
> 그리고, 나는 거기에서 나무들을 봤어요.
> 나중에 나는 소나무들
> 사진을 찍었어요.

_____

_____

_____

mountain 산   **pine tree** 소나무

CHECK!
CHECK!   ☐ 첫 글자는 대문자로 썼나요?   ☐ 구두점은 찍었나요?   ☐ 단어와 단어 사이는 띄어 썼나요?

Unit 04 Talking About Fairy Tales

동화에 대해 말하기

Read to Write

1 **Once upon a time,** there lived a rabbit and a turtle. 옛날 옛적에 토끼와 거북이가 살았어요. [주제]

2 **One day,** they ran a race. 어느 날, 그들은 경주를 했어요. [세부사항 1]

3 **In the end,** the turtle won the race. [세부사항 2]
결국 거북이가 경주에서 이겼어요.

Step 0 패턴 이해하기

1 주인공은 누구인가요? ⇒ **Once upon a time,** + there lived a rabbit and a turtle.
Once upon a time은 '옛날 옛적에', there lived ~는 '~가 살았다'란 의미예요.

2 무엇을 했나요? ⇒ **One day,** + they ran a race.
One day는 '어느 날'이라는 의미예요. 보통 이야기에서 어떤 사건이 시작되는 걸 나타내요. ran는 run(달리다)의 과거형으로, ran a race는 '경주를 했다'라는 의미예요.

3 결말은 어땠나요? ⇒ **In the end,** + the turtle won the race.
In the end는 '결국, 마침내'라는 의미예요. won은 win(이기다)의 과거형이에요.

Step 1 표현 파악하기 듣고, 따라 말해 보세요.

1
Cinderella
신데렐라
⇩

2
wanted to go to a ball
무도회에 가기를 원했다
⇩

3
the fairy godmother helped
요정 대모가 도왔다

4
Alice
앨리스
⇩

5
fell into a hole
구멍에 빠졌다
⇩

6
it was all a dream
전부 꿈이었다

Step 2 패턴 문장 뼈대 잡기

A 듣고, 따라 말한 후 완전한 문장을 써 보세요.

1		Once upon a time,	+	there lived a girl named Cinderella.
2		One day,	+	she wanted to go to a ball.
3		In the end,	+	the fairy godmother helped her.

4		Once upon a time,	+	there lived a girl named Alice.
5		One day,	+	she fell into a hole.
6		In the end,	+	it was all a dream.

B 듣고, 문장의 빈칸을 채운 후 전체 문장을 다시 써 보세요.

1 _____ upon a time, there lived a girl named Cinderella. ⇨

2 Once upon a time, _____ a girl named Alice. ⇨

3 _____, she wanted to go to a ball. ⇨

4 One day, _____ a hole. ⇨

5 _____, the fairy godmother helped her. ⇨

6 In the end, _____ a dream. ⇨

A 주어진 말을 바르게 배열해 문장을 완성하세요. 듣고, 문장 확인 후 뜻을 써 보세요.

1 there lived / Once upon a time, / ⇨
three little pigs

2 built / One day, / their own houses / they ⇨

3 was the best of them / In the end, / ⇨
the third pig's house

4 Once upon a time, / a boy named Jack / ⇨
there lived

5 climbed / One day, / a beanstalk / he ⇨

6 he / In the end, / rich / became ⇨

(New Words) **built** 지었다 | **climbed** 올라갔다 | **beanstalk** 콩나무 줄기

B 그림을 보고, 주어진 단어와 표현을 이용해 문장을 써 보세요.

옛날 옛적에 골디락스(Goldilocks)라는
한 소녀가 살았어요.
어느 날, 그녀는 곰 세 마리 집
(the Three Bears' house)에 들어갔어요.
마침내 그들이 집에 왔고,
그녀는 도망갔어요.

entered 들어갔다   **came home** 집에 왔다   **ran away** 도망갔다

CHECK! ☐ 첫 글자는 대문자로 썼나요?   ☐ 구두점은 찍었나요?   ☐ 단어와 단어 사이는 띄어 썼나요?
CHECK!

A 우리말에 맞게 빈칸에 알맞은 단어를 골라 써 보세요.

1 어느 날, 나는 정원에 갔어요. 그리고 나는 거기에서 곤충을 몇 마리 봤어요.

One day, I went to the _____. Then, I saw some _____ there.

garden / zoo   insects / animals

2 옛날 옛적에 토끼와 거북이가 살았어요.

_____ upon a time, _____ lived a rabbit and a turtle.

Once / First   they / there

3 맨 먼저, 옷을 치워요. 두 번째로, 침대를 정리해요.

First, _____ your clothes away. Second, _____ the bed.

put / take   switch / make

B 질문에 알맞은 답을 <보기>에서 골라 써 보세요.

1 How do you use a vacuum cleaner? ⇨

당신은 진공청소기를 어떻게 사용하나요?

2 How do you get there?   ⇨

당신은 거기에 어떻게 가나요?

3 Where did you go?   ⇨

당신은 어디에 갔었나요?

4 How does the fairy tale start?   ⇨

그 동화는 어떻게 시작하나요?

5 What happened to her?   ⇨

그녀에게 무슨 일이 생겼나요?

보기

I take the subway.   She fell into a hole.   I went to a city.
Plug the power cord into an outlet.   Once upon a time, there lived a girl named Alice.

C 주어진 말을 바르게 배열해 완전한 문장을 써 보세요.

1 on the power / switch / Second, ⇨

2 go straight / Last, / to the police station ⇨

3 some buildings / saw / I / Then, / there ⇨

4 took / I / pictures of skyscrapers / Later, ⇨

5 they / a race / One day, / ran ⇨

6 a shopping list / make / First, ⇨

D 문장을 보고, <u>틀린</u> 부분을 알맞게 고쳐 보세요.

1 in the end, He bEcame rich. ⇨

마침내 그는 부자가 되었어요.

2 one day, i wented to A mountain. ⇨

어느 날, 나는 산에 갔어요.

3 first, walks To the end oF the road. ⇨

먼저, 길 끝까지 걸어가세요.

4 Next, Crossing the rOad. ⇨

다음에, 길을 건너세요.

5 last, GO Grocery shopping. ⇨

마지막으로 쇼핑을 가세요.

6 once upon a time, There Lived a girl named ⇨

Cinderella. 옛날 옛적에 신데렐라라는 한 소녀가 살았어요.

Unit 05 Getting Ready for Outdoor Activities
야외 활동 준비하기

Read to Write

1 **First, I put on** a raincoat and boots.   [순서 1]
우선, 나는 비옷을 입고 장화를 신어요.

2 **Next, I get** an umbrella. 그 다음에, 나는 우산을 챙겨요.   [순서 2]

3 **Then, I go to** a park.   [순서 3]
그러고 나서 나는 공원에 가요.

Step 0 패턴 이해하기

1 무엇을 입나요?   ⇨ **First, + I put on** + a raincoat and boots.

First는 '우선, 맨 먼저'라는 의미예요. put on은 '(옷을) 입다, (신발을) 신다, (모자를) 쓰다'라는 뜻으로 쓰여요.

2 무엇을 가지고 가나요?   ⇨ **Next, + I get** + an umbrella.

Next는 '그 다음에', get은 '~을 가져가다'라는 의미예요.

3 어디에 가나요?   ⇨ **Then, + I go to** + a park.

Then은 '그리고, 그러고 나서', go to는 '~에 가다'라는 의미예요.

Step 1 표현 파악하기   듣고, 따라 말해 보세요.

1
a coat and a hat
코트와 모자
⇩

4
sunglasses
선글라스
⇩

2
gloves
장갑
⇩

5
a tube
튜브
⇩

3
the playground
놀이터

6
the sea
바다

A 듣고, 따라 말한 후 완전한 문장을 써 보세요.

1

First, + I put on + a coat and a hat.

2
Next, + I get + gloves.

3
Then, + I go to + the playground.

4

First, + I put on + sunglasses.

5
Next, + I get + a tube.

6
Then, + I go to + the sea.

B 듣고, 문장의 빈칸을 채운 후 전체 문장을 다시 써 보세요.

1 _____ , _____ a coat and a hat. ⇨

2 First, _____ . ⇨

3 _____ , _____ gloves. ⇨

4 Next, _____ . ⇨

5 _____ , _____ to the playground. ⇨

6 Then, _____ the sea. ⇨

A 주어진 말을 바르게 배열해 문장을 완성하세요. 듣고, 문장 확인 후 뜻을 써 보세요.

1 I / First, / hiking boots / put on ⇨

2 Next, / get / I / a backpack ⇨

3 go to / Then, / a mountain / I ⇨

4 First, / put on / I / a swimsuit ⇨

5 Next, / I / swimming goggles / get ⇨

6 I / Then, / a swimming pool / go to ⇨

New Words hiking boots 등산화 ｜ backpack 배낭 ｜ swimming goggles 물안경

B 그림을 보고, 주어진 단어를 이용해 문장을 써 보세요.

우선, 나는 운동복을 입어요.
그 다음에, 줄넘기를 챙겨요.
그러고 나서 나는 공원에 가요.

sweatsuit 운동복   jump rope 줄넘기

CHECK! CHECK! ☐ 첫 글자는 대문자로 썼나요? ☐ 구두점은 찍었나요? ☐ 단어와 단어 사이는 띄어 썼나요?

Unit 06 Talking About Future Plans
앞으로 할 일 말하기

 221

Read to Write

1 **First, I am going to** a flower shop.　　[순서 1]
우선, 나는 꽃집에 갈 거예요.

2 **Then, I am going to** buy flowers.　　[순서 2]
그러고 나서, 나는 꽃을 살 거예요.

3 **Last, I am going to** give them to my mom.　　[순서 3]
마지막으로 나는 그것을 엄마한테 드릴 거예요.

Step 0　패턴 이해하기

1 어디에 갈 건가요?　　⇒ **First, + I am going to** + a flower shop.
First는 '우선', 'I am going to + 장소'는 '나는 ~에 갈 거다'라는 의미예요.

2 무엇을 살 건가요?　　⇒ **Then, + I am going to** + buy flowers.
Then은 '그러고 나서'라는 의미예요. 'I am going to + 동사원형'은 '나는 ~할 거다'라는 의미로, 앞으로 할 일을 나타내요.

3 무엇을 할 건가요?　　⇒ **Last, + I am going to** + give them to my mom.
Last는 '마지막으로', give A to B는 'B에게 A를 주다'라는 의미예요.

Step 1　표현 파악하기　듣고, 따라 말해 보세요.

 222

1
a movie theater
영화 극장
⇩

2
buy a ticket and snacks
표와 간식을 사다
⇩

3
watch a movie
영화를 보다

4
a café
카페
⇩

5
buy a hot chocolate
핫 초콜릿을 사다
⇩

6
drink it
그것을 마시다

A 듣고, 따라 말한 후 완전한 문장을 써 보세요.

1 First, + I am going to + a movie theater.

2 Then, + I am going to + buy a ticket and snacks.

3 Last, + I am going to + watch a movie.

4 First, + I am going to + a café.

5 Then, + I am going to + buy a hot chocolate.

6 Last, + I am going to + drink it.

B 듣고, 문장의 빈칸을 채운 후 전체 문장을 다시 써 보세요.

1 _____ , _____ going to a movie theater. ⇨

2 First, _____ a café. ⇨

3 _____ , I _____ to buy a ticket and snacks. ⇨

4 Then, _____ buy a hot chocolate. ⇨

5 _____ , I _____ watch a movie. ⇨

6 Last, _____ drink it. ⇨

A 주어진 말을 바르게 배열해 문장을 완성하세요. 듣고, 문장 확인 후 뜻을 써 보세요.

1 I / First, / a bookstore / am going to ⇨ _____

_____

2 Then, / am going to / buy a book / I ⇨ _____

_____

3 I / am going to / Last, / read it ⇨ _____

_____

4 am going to / I / a clothing store / First, ⇨ _____

_____

5. am going to / I / Then, / buy a T-shirt ⇨ _____

_____

6 I / Last, / wear it / am going to ⇨ _____

_____

(New Words) bookstore 서점 ǀ clothing store 옷 가게

B 그림을 보고, 주어진 단어를 이용해 문장을 써 보세요.

우선, 나는 장난감 가게에 갈 거예요.
그러고 나서, 나는 장난감 차를 살 거예요.
마지막으로 그것으로 가지고 놀 거예요.

_____

_____

_____

toy store 장난감 가게　　**toy car** 장난감 차

 CHECK! CHECK! ☐ 첫 글자는 대문자로 썼나요?　☐ 구두점은 찍었나요?　☐ 단어와 단어 사이는 띄어 썼나요?

Unit 07 Making Desserts 디저트 만들기

Read to Write　　　How to make a fruit salad 과일 샐러드 만드는 법

1. **First, peel** fruits. 첫 번째, 과일들의 껍질을 벗기세요.　　[순서 1]

2. **Then, cut** them into pieces.　　[순서 2]
그리고 나서, 그것들을 잘게 잘라요.

3. **Last, mix** the fruit salad. Enjoy!　　[순서 3]
마지막으로 과일 샐러드를 섞어요. 맘껏 즐겨요!

Step 0 패턴 이해하기

1. 먼저 무엇을 하나요? ⇨ **First,** + **peel** + fruits.
peel은 '벗기다'라는 의미예요.

2. 그 다음은 무엇을 하나요? ⇨ **Then,** + **cut** + them into pieces.
pieces는 '(작게 자른 것의) 조각들'이라는 뜻이에요. 그래서 cut ~ into pieces는 '~을 작은 조각으로 썰다'라는 의미예요.

3. 마지막으로 무엇을 하나요? ⇨ **Last,** + **mix** + the fruit salad. + Enjoy!
mix는 '섞다', enjoy는 '마음껏 즐기다'라는 의미예요.

Step 1 표현 파악하기　듣고, 따라 말해 보세요.

1
put ice cream in a bowl
그릇에 아이스크림을 담다
⇩

2
add whipped cream and cherries
휘핑 크림과 체리를 더하다
⇩

3
sprinkle peanuts on top
맨 위에 땅콩을 뿌리다

4
mix flour and eggs
밀가루와 달걀을 섞다
⇩

5
add sugar and butter
설탕과 버터를 더하다
⇩

6
bake a cake
케이크를 굽다

A 듣고, 따라 말한 후 완전한 문장을 써 보세요.

How to make a sundae 선데이 아이스크림 만드는 법

1

| First, | + | put | + | ice cream in a bowl. |

2

| Then, | + | add | + | whipped cream and cherries. |

3

| Last, | + | sprinkle | + | peanuts on top. | + | Enjoy! |

How to make a cake 케이크 만드는 법

4

| First, | + | mix | + | flour and eggs. |

5

| Then, | + | add | + | sugar and butter. |

6

| Last, | + | bake | + | a cake. | + | Enjoy! |

B 듣고, 문장의 빈칸을 채운 후 전체 문장을 다시 써 보세요.

1 _____ , _____ in a bowl. ⇨

2 First, _____ and eggs. ⇨

3 _____ , _____ whipped cream and cherries. ⇨

4 Then, _____ and butter. ⇨

5 _____ , _____ peanuts on top. Enjoy! ⇨

6 Last, _____ . Enjoy! ⇨

A 주어진 말을 바르게 배열해 문장을 완성하세요. 듣고, 문장 확인 후 뜻을 써 보세요.

How to make orange juice 오렌지 주스 만드는 법

1 squeeze / First, / some oranges into a glass ⇨ _____

2 add / sugar to it / Then, ⇨ _____

3 Last, / it / well / stir ⇨ _____

How to make a milkshake 밀크세이크 만드는 법

4 First, / milk and ice cream / pour / into a cup ⇨ _____

5 Then, / the ingredients / blend ⇨ _____

6 top with / Last, / and some chocolate whipped cream ⇨ _____

(New Words) squeeze 짜다 I add 추가하다 I stir 젓다 I ingredient 재료 I blend 섞다 I top ~ 위에 얹다

B 그림을 보고, 주어진 단어를 이용해 문장을 써 보세요.

먼저, 그릇에 시리얼을 좀 부어요.
그러고 나서, 그것에 우유를 추가해요.
마지막으로 토핑들을 약간
추가해서 먹어요. 맘껏 즐기세요!

How to eat cereal 시리얼 먹는 법

_____

_____

cereal 시리얼   topping 토핑, 고명

CHECK!
CHECK!   ☐ 첫 글자는 대문자로 썼나요?   ☐ 구두점은 찍었나요?   ☐ 단어와 단어 사이는 띄어 썼나요?

Unit 08 How to Save the Earth 지구를 구하는 방법

Read to Write

① **First, I can** turn off the lights. [방법 1]
첫 번째, 나는 불을 끌 수 있어요.

② **Second, I can** reuse old clothes. [방법 2]
두 번째, 나는 헌 옷을 재사용할 수 있어요.

③ **Last, I can** recycle bottles. [방법 3]
마지막으로 나는 병을 재활용할 수 있어요.

Step 0 패턴 이해하기

① 지구를 위해 무엇을
할 수 있나요? ⇨ **First, I can** + turn off the lights.
can은 '~할 수 있다'라는 의미로, can 다음에는 동사원형이 와요. turn off는 '~을
끄다'라는 의미예요. 반대로 '~을 켜다'는 turn on을 써요.

② 또 무엇을 할 수 있나요? ⇨ **Second, I can** + reuse old clothes.
're-(다시) + use(사용하다)'가 합쳐진 reuse는 '재사용하다'라는 의미예요. 입던
옷을 리폼해서 입거나 가방 등으로 만들 때 reuse를 쓸 수 있어요.

③ 무엇이 더 있을까요? ⇨ **Last, I can** + recycle bottles.
recycle은 '~을 재활용하다'라는 의미예요.

Step 1 표현 파악하기 듣고, 따라 말해 보세요.

1
ride a bike
자전거를 타다
⇩

2
reuse old furniture
헌 가구를 재사용하다
⇩

3
recycle glass
유리를 재활용하다

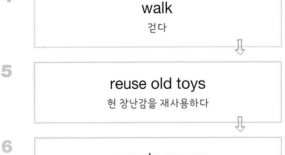

4
walk
걷다
⇩

5
reuse old toys
헌 장난감을 재사용하다
⇩

6
recycle paper
종이를 재활용하다

A 듣고, 따라 말한 후 완전한 문장을 써 보세요.

1 First, I can   +   ride a bike.

2 Second, I can   +   reuse old furniture.

3 Last, I can   +   recycle glass.

4 First, I can   +   walk.

5 Second, I can   +   reuse old toys.

6 Last, I can   +   recycle paper.

B 듣고, 문장의 빈칸을 채운 후 전체 문장을 다시 써 보세요.

1 _____ , _____ ride a bike.   ⇨

2 First, _____ .   ⇨

3 _____ , _____ reuse old furniture. ⇨

4 Second, _____ old toys.   ⇨

5 _____ , _____ recycle glass.   ⇨

6 Last, _____ paper.   ⇨

A 주어진 말을 바르게 배열해 문장을 완성하세요. 듣고, 문장 확인 후 뜻을 써 보세요.

235

1 I / First, / ride a bus / can ⇨ _____

2 I / Second, / reuse old books / can ⇨ _____

3 I / can / Last, / recycle cans ⇨ _____

4 can / carpool / First, / I ⇨ _____

5 can / I / Second, / reuse old batteries ⇨ _____

6 can / I / Last, / recycle boxes ⇨ _____

New Words carpool 카풀(승용차 함께 타기)을 하다 ㅣ battery 배터리

B 그림을 보고, 주어진 단어와 표현을 이용해 문장을 써 보세요.

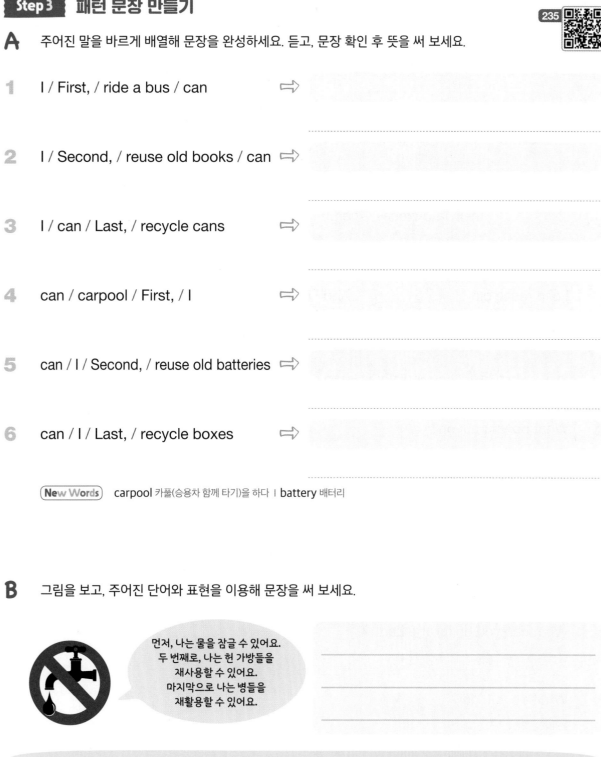

먼저, 나는 물을 잠글 수 있어요.
두 번째로, 나는 헌 가방들을
재사용할 수 있어요.
마지막으로 나는 병들을
재활용할 수 있어요.

_____

_____

_____

turn off the water 물을 잠그다   old bag 헌 가방   bottle 병

 CHECK! CHECK!   ☐ 첫 글자는 대문자로 썼나요?   ☐ 구두점은 찍었나요?   ☐ 단어와 단어 사이는 띄어 썼나요?

A 우리말에 맞게 빈칸에 알맞은 단어를 골라 써 보세요.

1 나는 영화관에 갈 거예요. 그리고 나서, 나는 영화를 볼 거예요.

I am going to a _____. Then, I am going to _____ a movie.

movie theater / bookstore   give / watch

2 그것들을 잘게 잘라요. 그리고 나서, 과일 샐러드를 섞어요. 맘껏 즐겨요!

_____ them into pieces. Then, _____ the fruit salad. Enjoy!

Cut / Scoop   add / mix

3 나는 헌 가구를 재사용할 수 있어요. 그리고 나는 유리를 재활용할 수 있어요.

I can reuse old _____. And I can recycle _____.

furniture / clothes   cans / glass

B 질문에 알맞은 답을 <보기>에서 골라 써 보세요.

1 What do you put on?   ⇨

당신은 무엇을 입나요?

2 What are you going to do?   ⇨

당신은 무엇을 할 예정인가요?

3 What should I do first?   ⇨

내가 무엇을 먼저 해야 하나요?

4 What can you do for the Earth?   ⇨

당신은 지구를 위해서 무엇을 할 수 있나요?

5 What do you get?   ⇨

당신은 무엇을 가지고 가나요?

보기

I am going to buy flowers.   First, peel fruits.   I can turn off the lights.
I get an umbrella.   I put on a raincoat and boots.

C 주어진 말을 바르게 배열해 완전한 문장을 써 보세요.

1 a playground / I / go to ⇨

2 can / a bike / I / ride ⇨

3 cake / a / Bake ⇨

4 ice cream / Put / in a bowl ⇨

5 am going to / I / a café ⇨

6 put on / I / hiking boots ⇨

D 문장을 보고, <u>틀린</u> 부분을 알맞게 고쳐 보세요.

1 i goed To a swimming pool. ⇨

나는 수영장에 가요.

2 I gets A jump rope. ⇨

나는 줄넘기를 가져가요.

3 i is Going to A toy store. ⇨

나는 장난감 가게에 갈 거예요.

4 add some milk To it. ⇨

거기에 우유를 약간 추가하세요.

5 pours Some cereal Into a bowl. ⇨

그릇에 시리얼을 좀 부으세요.

6 I cans Recycle bottles. ⇨

나는 병을 재활용할 수 있어요.

5. It looks like a ladybug. 그것은 무당벌레처럼 생겼어요.

6. It has spots on its back. 그것은 등에 점이 있어요.

B　Here is a bag. It looks like a panda. It has a big pocket.

Unit 01　Describing Animals　pp. 13~14

Step 2

B　1. This is → This is an alligator.

2. This is a pig → This is a pig.

3. It has → It has a long tail.

4. has, eyes, tail
→ It has two small eyes and a short tail.

5. is green → It is green.

6. It is pink → It is pink.

Step 3

A　1. This is a giraffe. 이것은 기린이에요.

2. It has a long neck and four legs.
그것은 긴 목에 다리가 네 개예요.

3. It is yellow and brown. 그것은 노랗고 갈색이에요.

4. This is a penguin. 이것은 펭귄이에요.

5. It has two short legs. 그것은 짧은 두 다리를 가지고 있어요.

6. It is black and white. 그것은 검고 하얗죠.

B　This is a parrot. It has feathers. It is yellow and blue.

Unit 02　Describing My Things　pp. 16~17

Step 2

B　1. Here is → Here is a wizard hat.

2. is a toy → Here is a toy octopus.

3. It looks like → It looks like a cone.

4. looks like → It looks like an alien.

5. It has → It has stars and a moon.

6. has, head, eight → It has a head and eight tentacles.

Step 3

A　1. Here is a cool kite. 여기 멋진 연이 있어요.

2. It looks like a bat. 그것은 박쥐처럼 생겼어요.

3. It has two big wings.
그것은 두 개의 큰 날개를 가지고 있어요.

4. Here is a new mouse. 여기 새 (컴퓨터) 마우스가 있어요.

Unit 03　Describing My Friends　pp. 19~20

Step 2

B　1. He is → He is my friend Jack.

2. is my friend → She is my friend Sandy.

3. He has → He has green eyes and a round face.

4. has dimples, hair → She has dimples and curly hair.

5. He is → He is very funny.

6. is, curious → She is very curious.

Step 3

A　1. She is my friend Emma. 그녀는 내 친구 엠마예요.

2. She has long hair and a round face.
그녀는 머리가 길고 얼굴이 둥글어요.

3. She is very friendly. 그녀는 아주 다정해요.

4. He is my friend Tom. 그는 내 친구 톰이에요.

5. He has a big mouth and dark hair.
그는 입이 크고 머리가 어두운 색이에요.

6. He is a little bit shy. 그는 조금 수줍어해요.

B　He is my friend Joey. He has short hair and blue eyes. He is very brave.

Unit 04　Describing My Family　pp. 22~23

Step 2

B　1. He is → He is my brother.

2. is my grandmother → She is my grandmother.

3. He is wearing → He is wearing blue jeans.

4. She is wearing → She is wearing a dress.

5. He looks → He looks fantastic.

6. She looks lovely → She looks lovely.

Step 3

A　1. She is my mom. 그녀는 나의 엄마예요.

2. She is wearing pants. 그녀는 바지를 입고 있어요.

3. She looks young. 그녀는 젊어 보여요.

4. He is my uncle. 그는 나의 삼촌이에요.

5. He is wearing a coat. 그는 코트를 입고 있어요.

6. He looks great. 그는 멋져 보여요.

B He is my dad. He is wearing a suit. He looks great.

Unit 05 | **Describing Jobs** | pp. 25~26

Step 2

B 1. They are → They are zookeepers.
2. are photographers → We are photographers.
3. They work → They work at the zoo.
4. work at → We work at a studio.
5. They take care of → They take care of animals.
6. We take pictures → We take pictures.

Step 3

A 1. They are mechanics. 그들은 정비사들이에요.
2. They work at the airport. 그들은 공항에서 일해요.
3. They fix airplanes. 그들은 비행기를 수리해요.
4. We are police officers. 우리는 경찰관들이에요.
5. We work at the police station.
우리는 경찰서에서 일해요.
6. We catch thieves. 우리는 도둑들을 잡아요.

B We are mail carriers. We work at the post office. We deliver letters to people.

01 **Review Test** pp. 27~28

A 1. elephant, gray
2. bag, pocket
3. chefs, restaurant

B 1. This is a pig.
2. It looks like a cone.
3. She is very funny.
4. He is my brother.
5. She is wearing pants.

C 1. It has a long tail.
2. It is pink.
3. Here is a new mouse.
4. She is wearing blue jeans.
5. We are mail carriers.
6. We deliver letters to people.

D 1. We work at the post office.
2. They **are** mechanics.
3. **He is** my dad.
4. **She is** wearing **a** coat.
5. He **has** short hair and blue eyes.
6. She **is** a little bit shy.

Unit 06 | **Describing Actions 1** | pp. 30~31

Step 2

B 1. play basketball → I play basketball after school.
2. play the piano → I play the piano after school.
3. throw → I throw the ball.
4. I read → I read music.
5. I, jump → I also jump high.
6. also touch, keyboard → I also touch the keyboard.

Step 3

A 1. I learn yoga after school. 나는 방과 후에 요가를 배워요.
2. I breathe properly. 나는 바르게 숨을 쉬죠.
3. I also stand on one leg. 나는 또 한 발로 서요.
4. I dance after school. 나는 방과 후에 춤을 춰요.
5. I shake my body. 나는 몸을 흔들죠.
6. I also stretch my arms. 나는 또 팔을 뻗어요.

B I play baseball after school. I hit the ball. I also catch the ball.

Unit 07 | **Describing Actions 2** | pp. 33~34

Step 2

B 1. My dad is → My dad is in the kitchen.
2. am in, room → I am in my room.
3. cutting → He is cutting some onions and mushrooms.
4. am throwing away → I am throwing away the garbage.
5. He is cooking → He is cooking ramen, too.
6. I am sweeping → I am sweeping the floor, too.

Step 3

A 1. My sisters are in the living room.
우리 언니들은 거실에 있어요.
2. They are watching a movie. 그들은 영화를 보고 있어요.
3. They are eating popcorn, too. 그들은 팝콘도 먹고 있어요.

4. My grandmother is in her bedroom.
   나의 할머니는 침실에 계세요.

5. She is listening to music. 그녀는 음악을 듣고 있어요.

6. She is writing a letter, too. 그녀는 편지도 쓰고 있어요.

B My brother is in the bathroom. He is washing his face. He is brushing his teeth, too.

Unit 08 **Describing My Town** pp. 36~37

Step 2

B 1. live in → I live in the countryside.

2. seaside town → I live in a beautiful seaside town.

3. There are → There are a lot of trees and plants.

4. There are, yachts → There are a lot of yachts.

5. There is → There is a beautiful lake.

6. There is, lighthouse → There is a red lighthouse.

Step 3

A 1. I live in a peaceful town. 나는 평화로운 마을에 살아요.

2. There are a lot of blue houses. 파란 집들이 많아요.

3. There is a high mountain. 높은 산이 있어요.

4. I live in a forest. 나는 숲에 살아요.

5. There are a lot of huts. 오두막들이 많아요.

6. There is a tall waterfall. 높은 폭포가 있어요.

B I live in the desert. There are a lot of camels. There is an oasis.

Unit 09 **Describing My House** pp. 39~40

Step 2

B 1. This is → This is my sister's bedroom.

2. is the kitchen → This is the kitchen.

3. does her → She does her homework every afternoon.

4. cooks meals → My mom cooks meals for my family.

5. play, there → She and I sometimes play a board game there.

6. eat, there → We usually eat together there.

Step 3

A 1. This is our yard. 여기는 우리 마당이에요.

2. My dad reads a book. 우리 아빠는 책을 읽어요.

3. My family sometimes has dinner there.
   우리 가족은 가끔 거기서 저녁을 먹어요.

4. This is the bathroom. 여기는 욕실이에요.

5. My family washes our hands and faces.
   우리 가족은 손과 얼굴을 씻죠.

6. I always brush my teeth there.
   나는 항상 거기서 이를 닦아요.

B This is the attic. My mom writes there. My mom and I sometimes play chess there.

02 Review Test pp. 41~42

A 1. soccer, pass

2. kitchen, cooking

3. seaside, lighthouse

B 1. I play the piano after school.

2. My mom is in the garden.

3. I live in a big city.

4. This is the living room.

5. My dad cooks meals for my family there.

C 1. This is my sister's bedroom.

2. She does her homework every afternoon.

3. There are a lot of yachts.

4. I live in the desert.

5. He is washing his face.

6. I also touch the keyboard.

D 1. I jump high.

2. My sisters are in the living room.

3. They are watching a movie.

4. She is writing a letter.

5. There is a long bridge.

6. We always eat together there.

Unit 10 **Describing Food** pp. 44~45

Step 2

B 1. Look at → Look at the lemon.

2. at, potato chips → Look at the potato chips.

3. It tastes → It tastes sour and juicy.

4. taste salty, crispy → They taste salty and crispy.

5. It is yellow → It is yellow and oval.

6. They are beige, thin → They are beige and thin.

Step 3

A 1. Look at the pizza. 피자를 보세요.

2. It tastes salty and sweet. 그것은 짜고 달아요.

3. It is round and thin. 그것은 둥글고 얇아요.

4. Look at the ice cream. 아이스크림을 보세요.

5. It tastes sweet and creamy. 그것은 달고 크림 같아요.

6. It is cold and soft. 그것은 차갑고 부드러워요.

B Look at the chicken nuggets. They taste crispy and delicious. They are round and chewy.

Unit 11 Describing Toys   pp. 47~48

Step 2

B 1. I see → I see an action figure.

2. see a toy → I see a toy.

3. It looks like → It looks like a movie star.

4. looks like, cowboy → It looks like a cowboy.

5. It is wearing → It is wearing a blue mask.

6. It is wearing jeans → It is wearing jeans.

Step 3

A 1. I see a robot. 로봇이 보여요.

2. It looks like a dog. 그것은 개처럼 생겼어요.

3. It is wearing sunglasses. 그것은 선글라스를 쓰고 있어요.

4. I see a nice doll. 멋있는 인형이 보여요.

5. It looks like an astronaut. 그것은 우주 비행사처럼 보여요.

6. It is wearing a spacesuit. 그것은 우주복을 입고 있어요.

B I see an action figure. It looks like a superhero. It is wearing a cape.

Unit 12 Describing People's Activities

pp. 50~51

Step 2

B 1. are under → A man and a woman are under the tree.

2. tennis court → A man and a girl are on the tennis court.

3. are sitting → They are sitting on a bench.

4. is serving first → He is serving first.

5. They are looking at → They are looking at flowers.

6. She is hitting → She is hitting the ball.

Step 3

A 1. A woman is in a dog park.
한 여자가 개 공원에 있어요.

2. She is jogging with a dog. 그녀는 강아지와 함께 조깅을 하고 있어요.

3. She is listening to music. 그녀는 음악을 듣고 있어요.

4. Two boys are in the woods. 두 명의 소년이 숲속에 있어요.

5. They are birdwatching. 그들은 새를 관찰하고 있어요.

6. They are holding binoculars. 그들은 쌍안경을 들고 있어요.

B A man is in front of a cage. He is taking pictures. He is feeding a tiger.

Unit 13 Describing Insects   pp. 53~54

Step 2

B 1. is on → A bee is on the flower.

2. is on → A dragonfly is on the branch.

3. It has → It has stripes.

4. has shiny wings → It has shiny wings.

5. It is eating → It is eating honey.

6. It is beating → It is beating its wings.

Step 3

A 1. A grasshopper is on the rock. 메뚜기가 바위 위에 있어요.

2. It has long antennae. 그것은 긴 더듬이가 있어요.

3. It is leaping great distances.
그것은 대단한 거리를 뛰고 있어요.

4. An ant is on the ground. 개미가 땅 위에 있어요.

5. It has six legs. 그것은 다리가 여섯 개예요.

6. It is carrying heavy loads.
그것은 무거운 짐을 운반하고 있어요.

B A ladybug is on the branch. It has black spots. It is crawling slowly.

A 1. princess, dress
   2. playing, singing
   3. wings, warming

B 1. It tastes sweet.
   2. I see a pretty doll.
   3. A woman and a baby are on the grass.
   4. It is on the leaf.
   5. It is round.

C 1. An ant is on the ground.
   2. It has black spots.
   3. A man and a girl are on a court.
   4. They are sitting on a bench.
   5. I see an action figure.
   6. It is wearing a cape.

D 1. Look at the pizza.
   2. It tastes cold and soft.
   3. It looks like a movie star.
   4. They are holding binoculars.
   5. It has six legs.
   6. She is listening to music.

PART 2 내가 좋아하는 것에 대해 쓰기

Unit 01 **My Favorite Friend**   pp. 59~60

Step 2

B 1. favorite friend → My favorite friend is Sally.
   2. favorite friend is → My favorite friend is Tom.
   3. She is → She is very quiet.
   4. is, funny → He is very funny.
   5. We, like to → We both like to read books.
   6. like to watch → We both like to watch movies.

Step 3

A 1. My favorite friend is Noah.
      내가 가장 좋아하는 친구는 노아예요.
   2. He is very talkative. 그는 아주 수다스럽죠.
   3. We both like to make jokes.
      우리는 둘 다 농담하는 것을 좋아해요.
   4. My favorite friend is Emma.
      내가 가장 좋아하는 친구는 엠마예요.
   5. She is very curious. 그녀는 호기심이 아주 많아요.
   6. We both like to play board games.
      우리 둘 다 보드게임하는 것을 좋아해요.

B My favorite friend is Liam. He is very smart. We both like to play computer games.

Unit 02 **My Favorite Snack**   pp. 62~63

Step 2

B 1. I really like → I really like gummy worms.
   2. like potato chips → I really like potato chips.
   3. soft, tender → They are soft and tender. Yummy!
   4. are crispy, Yummy → They are crispy. Yummy!
   5. There are → There are different shapes and sizes.
   6. There are many → There are many flavors.

Step 3

A 1. I really like dumplings. 나는 만두를 정말 좋아해요.
   2. They are juicy. Yummy!
      그것들은 육즙이 풍부하죠. 아주 맛있어요!
   3. There are a lot of ingredients.
      많은 재료가 (들어) 있어요.
   4. I really like pizza. 나는 피자를 정말 좋아해요.
   5. It is delicious. Yummy! 그것은 맛있어요. 아주 맛있어요!
   6. There are many flavors.
      여러 가지 맛이 있어요.

B I really like bagels. They are chewy. Yummy! There is a lot of cream cheese.

Unit 03 **My Favorite Superhero**   pp. 65~66

Step 2

B 1. My favorite → My favorite superhero is Flash.
   2. superhero is → My favorite superhero is the Hulk.

3. He is → He is funny and fast.

4. is big, strong → He is big and strong.

5. He can run → He can run faster than lightning.

6. smash bad men → He can smash bad men.

Step 3

A 1. My favorite superhero is Aquaman.
  내가 가장 좋아하는 슈퍼히어로는 아쿠아맨이에요.

2. He is strong and cool. 그는 힘이 세고 멋져요.

3. He can breathe underwater.
  그는 물속에서도 숨을 쉴 수 있어요.

4. My favorite superhero is Supergirl.
  내가 가장 좋아하는 슈퍼히어로는 슈퍼걸이에요.

5. She is kind-hearted. 그녀는 인정이 많아요.

6. She can fly in the sky. 그녀는 하늘을 날 수 있어요.

B My favorite superhero is Ironman. He is very smart and amazing. He can solve problems and help people.

Unit 04 My Favorite Subject
pp. 68~69

Step 2

B 1. Social studies → Social studies is my favorite subject.

2. favorite subject → Music is my favorite subject.

3. I am → I am really curious.

4. am, joyful → I am really joyful.

5. like to → I like to learn about cultures and societies.

6. like to play → I like to play the piano.

Step 3

A 1. Art is my favorite subject.
  미술은 내가 가장 좋아하는 과목이에요.

2. I am really creative. 나는 정말 창의적이에요.

3. I like to draw pictures. 나는 그림 그리는 것을 좋아해요.

4. English is my favorite subject.
  영어는 내가 가장 좋아하는 과목이에요.

5. I am really talkative. 나는 정말 수다스러워요.

6. I like to talk with friends in English.
  나는 친구들과 영어로 이야기하는 것을 좋아해요.

B Math is my favorite subject. I am really smart. I like to solve math problems.

Unit 05 My Favorite Holiday
pp. 71~72

Step 2

B 1. Halloween is → Halloween is an exciting day.

2. is a joyful → New Year's Day is a joyful day.

3. I wear → I wear a costume like a movie star.

4. watch a parade → I watch a parade.

5. feel excited → I feel excited.

6. I feel great → I feel great.

Step 3

A 1. Valentine's Day is a wonderful day.
  밸런타인데이는 멋진 날이에요.

2. I exchange cards and gifts with friends.
  나는 친구들과 카드와 선물을 교환해요.

3. I feel excited. 나는 신이 나요.

4. Thanksgiving Day is a great day.
  추수감사절은 대단한 날이에요.

5. I share delicious dishes with my family.
  나는 가족들과 맛있는 음식들을 나눠요.

6. I feel warm and grateful. 나는 따뜻함과 감사함을 느껴요.

B Mother's Day is a special day. I give gifts to Mom. [I give Mom gifts] I feel grateful and happy.

04 Review Test
pp. 73~74

A 1. P.E., energetic

2. happy, get

3. brave and kind, climb

B 1. My favorite friend is Ben.

2. It is super sweet.

3. He can run faster than lightning.

4. I like to play soccer.

5. I feel happy.

C 1. She is kind-hearted.

2. My favorite superhero is Supergirl.

3. I am really creative.

4. He can smash bad men.

5. I watch a parade.

6. Halloween is an exciting day.

D
1. **I give** gifts to Mom.
2. He **is** strong and cool.
3. There **are** many ingredients.
4. I **like** to solve math problems.
5. She **can fly** in the sky.
6. We both **like** to **play** computer games.

Unit 06 **My Favorite Sport** pp. 76~77

Step 2

B
1. I like → I like soccer the most.
2. like, the most → I like swimming the most.
3. learn teamwork → I learn teamwork from my soccer team.
4. learn, from → I learn confidence from swimming.
5. What a → What a passionate sport!
6. What an incredible sport → What an incredible sport!

Step 3

A
1. I like figure skating the most.
   나는 피겨 스케이팅을 가장 좋아해요.
2. I learn balance from figure skating.
   나는 피겨 스케이팅에서 균형을 배워요.
3. What a skillful sport! 정말 기술적인 스포츠예요!
4. I like baseball the most. 나는 야구를 가장 좋아해요.
5. I learn teamwork from my baseball team.
   나는 야구팀에서 팀워크를 배워요.
6. What a cheerful sport! 정말 쾌활한 스포츠예요!

B I like volleyball the most. I learn teamwork from my volleyball team. What an exciting sport!

Unit 07 **My Favorite Season and Weather** pp. 79~80

Step 2

B
1. I think that → I think that summer is the best.
2. think that fall → I think that fall is the best.
3. It is hot → It is hot and humid.
4. is cool, windy → It is cool and windy.
5. It is good → It is good for going to the beach.
6. is good for taking → It is good for taking a walk.

Step 3

A
1. I think that winter is the best.
   나는 겨울이 최고인 것 같아요.
2. It is cold and dry. 춥고 건조하죠.
3. It is good for skiing and skating.
   스키와 스케이트 타기에 좋아요.
4. I think that sunny weather is the best.
   나는 화창한 날씨가 최고인 것 같아요.
5. It is pleasant and bright. 쾌적하고 밝죠.
6. It is good for having a picnic. 소풍 가기 좋아요.

B I think that snowy weather is the best. It is snowy and cold. It is good for making a snowman.

Unit 08 **My Favorite Day of the Week** pp. 82~83

Step 2

B
1. favorite day → My favorite day of the week is Monday.
2. day, week → My favorite day of the week is Wednesday.
3. have English → I have English class on Mondays.
4. have P.E., on → I have P.E. class on Wednesdays.
5. Speaking English is → Speaking English is really fun.
6. Playing sports, exciting → Playing sports is really exciting.

Step 3

A
1. My favorite day of the week is Thursday.
   내가 가장 좋아하는 요일은 목요일이에요.
2. I have a special cooking class on Thursdays.
   목요일마다 특별한 요리 수업이 있어요.
3. Making dessert is really enjoyable.
   디저트 만들기는 정말 즐거워요.
4. My favorite day of the week is Wednesday.
   내가 가장 좋아하는 요일은 수요일이에요.
5. I have robot class on Wednesdays.
   수요일마다 로봇 수업이 있어요.
6. Making a robot is really interesting.
   로봇 만들기는 정말 흥미로워요.

B My favorite day of the week is Saturday. I have no class on Saturdays. Sleeping late is really relaxing.

Unit 09   The Best Thing About Vacation
pp. 85~86

Step 2

B 1. Spring vacation → Spring vacation was super fun.
   2. vacation was super → Winter vacation was super fun.
   3. I went to → I went to the festival.
   4. went to the → I went to the ski resort.
   5. I enjoyed watching → I enjoyed watching the parade.
   6. I enjoyed skiing → I enjoyed skiing all day.

Step 3

A 1. Summer vacation was super fun.
   여름 방학이 정말 재미있었어요.
   2. I went to the pool. 나는 수영장에 갔어요.
   3. I enjoyed eating ice cream.
   나는 아이스크림 먹는 것을 즐겼어요.
   4. Spring vacation was super fun.
   봄 방학이 정말 재미있었어요.
   5. I went to the park. 나는 공원에 갔어요.
   6. I enjoyed seeing beautiful flowers.
   나는 아름다운 꽃들을 보는 걸 즐겼어요.

B Winter vacation was super fun. I went to the park. I enjoyed having a snowball fight.

05   Review Test
pp. 87~88

A 1. snowy, making
   2. P.E., exciting
   3. ski resort, skiing

B 1. I like the marathon the most.
   2. It is warm and breezy.
   3. I have art class on Tuesdays.
   4. I went to my grandma's house.
   5. Summer vacation was super fun.

C 1. I enjoyed eating ice cream.
   2. I have robot class on Wednesdays.
   3. Sleeping late is really relaxing.
   4. It is pleasant and bright.
   5. What an exciting sport!
   6. I learn teamwork from my soccer team.

D 1. It is good for enjoying outdoors.
   2. My favorite day of the week is Monday.
   3. Winter vacation was super fun.
   4. Drawing pictures is really enjoyable.
   5. I think that sunny weather is the best.
   6. I like baseball the most.

Unit 10   The Best Place in the City
pp. 90~91

Step 2

B 1. the best → Fun Toy Store is the best place in my city.
   2. the best place → Nari Tower is the best place in my city.
   3. It has, toys → It has interesting toys.
   4. has an observation deck → It has an observation deck.
   5. I can hold → I can hold and play with them.
   6. can enjoy → I can enjoy the city view at a glance.

Step 3

A 1. The National Museum is the best place in my city.
   국립박물관이 우리 도시에서 최고의 장소예요.
   2. It has many exhibitions. 그곳에는 많은 전시회가 있어요.
   3. I can look at pictures and sculptures.
   나는 그림과 조각품들을 관람할 수 있어요.
   4. The dog park is the best place in my city.
   개 공원이 우리 도시에서 최고의 장소예요.
   5. It has a large playground. 그곳에는 넓은 놀이터가 있어요.
   6. I can play with my dog. 나는 우리 개와 놀 수 있어요.

B Magic Amusement Park is the best place in my city. It has many fun rides. I can ride a Ferris wheel and a roller coaster.

Unit 11 The Best Movie

pp. 93~94

Step 2

B   1. really like → I really like *Superman*.

2. I really like → I really like *Avatar*.

3. It is an action → It is an action movie.

4. science fiction movie → It is a science fiction movie.

5. It is so → It is so thrilling.

6. is so interesting → It is so interesting.

Step 3

A   1. I really like *Hidden Figures*.
   나는 <히든 피겨스>를 정말 좋아해요.

2. It is a history movie. 그것은 역사 영화예요.

3. It is so touching. 그것은 아주 감동적이에요.

4. I really like *Up*. 나는 <업>을 정말 좋아해요.

5. It is an animated movie. 그것은 애니메이션 영화예요.

6. It is so sad. 그것은 정말 슬퍼요.

B   I really like *Matilda*. It is a musical movie. It is so exciting.

Unit 12 The Perfect Pet

pp. 96~97

Step 2

B   1. The perfect pet → The perfect pet for me is a cat.

2. pet, is → The perfect pet for me is a hamster.

3. Cats are playful → Cats are playful and independent.

4. are so adorable → Hamsters are so adorable.

5. I smile when → I smile when they hug me.

6. when, play → I laugh when they play in a cage.

Step 3

A   1. The perfect pet for me is a rabbit.
   나에게 딱 맞는 반려동물은 토끼예요.

2. Rabbits are adorable and fluffy.
   토끼들은 사랑스럽고 솜털로 뒤덮여 있어요.

3. I smile when they hop.
   그것들이 깡충 뛸 때 나는 미소를 지어요.

4. The perfect pet for me is a fish.
   나에게 딱 맞는 반려동물은 물고기예요.

5. Fish are incredibly beautiful.
   물고기들은 믿을 수 없을 만큼 아름다워요.

6. I smile when they swim gracefully.
   그것들이 우아하게 헤엄칠 때 나는 미소를 짓죠.

B   The perfect pet for me is a hedgehog. Hedgehogs are incredibly cute. I smile when they explore in a cage.

Unit 13 The Best Restaurant

pp. 99~100

Step 2

B   1. I really love → I really love the Chinese restaurant.

2. really love the → I really love the Japanese restaurant.

3. It is famous → It is famous for its dim sum.

4. is famous for its → It is famous for its sushi.

5. The dim sum → The dim sum is really juicy and tasty.

6. really fresh → The sushi is really fresh and healthy.

Step 3

A   1. I really love the chicken restaurant.
   나는 그 치킨집을 아주 좋아해요.

2. It is famous for its fried chicken.
   그곳은 프라이드 치킨으로 유명해요.

3. The fried chicken is really crispy and chewy.
   그 프라이드 치킨은 정말 바삭하고 쫄깃해요.

4. I really love the Indian restaurant.
   나는 그 인도 식당을 아주 좋아해요.

5. It is famous for its beef curry.
   그곳은 소고기 커리로 유명해요.

6. The beef curry is really spicy and yummy.
   그 소고기 커리는 정말 맵고 맛있어요.

B   I really love the Vietnamese restaurant. It is famous for its pho and spring rolls. The pho is really healthy and delicious.

Unit 14 My favorite Family Member

pp. 102~103

Step 2

B   1. My favorite → My favorite family member is my dad.

2. family member → My favorite family member is my grandmother.

3. He is wise → He is wise and strong.

4. is loving → She is loving and caring.

5. He, encourages me → He always encourages me.

6. cooks delicious → She always cooks delicious food.

Step 3

A 1. My favorite family member is my grandfather.
내가 가장 좋아하는 가족 구성원은 우리 할아버지예요.

2. He is knowledgeable and wise.
그는 아는 것이 많고 현명해요.

3. He always answers me. 그는 항상 나에게 대답해 줘요.

4. My favorite family member is my sister.
내가 가장 좋아하는 가족 구성원은 우리 언니예요.

5. She is kind and friendly. 그녀는 친절하고 다정하죠.

6. She always supports me. 그녀는 항상 나를 응원해 줘요.

B My favorite family member is my brother. He is adventurous and creative. He always enjoys challenges.

06 Review Test
pp. 104~105

A 1. Japanese, fresh and healthy

2. adorable, play

3. *Superman*, thrilling

B 1. Happy Shopping Mall is the best place in my city.

2. It is an animated movie.

3. The perfect pet for me is a dog.

4. It is famous for its seafood pizza.

5. My favorite family member is my mom.

C 1. It has a large playground.

2. I can enjoy the city view at a glance.

3. I really like *Hidden Figures*.

4. It is a history movie.

5. Dogs are incredibly loyal.

6. It is famous for its dim sum.

D 1. Nari Tower is the best place in my city.

2. It is so interesting.

3. I smile when they hug me.

4. The fried chicken is really crispy and chewy.

5. She is loving and caring.

6. He always enjoys challenges.

PART 3 온라인 글쓰기

Unit 01 Invitation Messages
pp. 109~110

Step 2

B 1. What are you → What are you doing tomorrow, Lora?

2. this Friday → What are you doing this Friday, Sarah?

3. Let's go → Let's go to the river.

4. to the zoo → Let's go to the zoo.

5. We can fish → We can fish in the river.

6. can see pandas → We can see pandas.

Step 3

A 1. What are you doing this Monday, Jin?
진아, 이번 주 월요일에 뭐 할 거야?

2. Let's go to the library. 같이 도서관에 가자.

3. We can read new books. 우리는 새 책들을 읽을 수 있어.

4. What are you doing this Wednesday, Chris?
크리스야, 이번 주 수요일에 뭐 할 거야?

5. Let's go to the beach. 해변에 같이 가자.

6. We can see fireworks. 우리는 불꽃놀이를 볼 수 있어.

B What are you doing this Tuesday, Tom? Let's go to the stadium. We can watch a baseball game.

Unit 02 Thank-You Messages
pp. 112~113

Step 2

B 1. Thank you → Thank you for the gloves, Uncle Tom.

2. the cap, Mom → Thank you for the cap, Mom.

3. The gloves are → The gloves are really fantastic.

4. is really terrific → The cap is really terrific.

5. You are so → You are so friendly.

6. are so awesome → You are so awesome.

A 1. Thank you for the jeans, Amy. 청바지 고마워, 에이미.

2. The jeans are really trendy.
   그 청바지 정말 최신 유행하는 거야.

3. You are so wonderful. 너는 정말 멋져.

4. Thank you for the jacket, Leo. 레오야, 재킷 고마워.

5. The jacket is really pretty. 그 재킷 너무 예뻐.

6. You are so nice. 너는 정말 다정해.

B Thank you for the sunglasses, Miguel. The sunglasses are really wonderful. You are so friendly.

Unit 03 **Looking for a Pet** pp. 115~116

Step 2

B 1. I am looking → I am looking for my cat, Molly.

2. my hamster → I am looking for my hamster, Tiny.

3. I lost her → I lost her at the bus stop.

4. lost him in → I lost him in this building.

5. She has a → She has a long tail and big eyes.

6. has red hair → He has red hair and black eyes.

Step 3

A 1. I am looking for my rabbit, Bunny.
   나는 내 토끼 버니를 찾고 있어요.

2. I lost her in the mall.
   나는 그것을 쇼핑몰에서 잃어버렸어요.

3. She has white fur and a short tail.
   그것은 하얀 털과 짧은 꼬리를 가지고 있어요.

4. I am looking for my hedgehog, Spike.
   나는 내 고슴도치 스파이크를 찾고 있어요.

5. I lost him in the playground.
   나는 그것을 놀이터에서 잃어버렸어요.

6. He has tiny eyes and sharp spines.
   그것은 아주 작은 눈과 뾰족한 가시들을 가지고 있어요.

B I am looking for my parrot, Cotton. I lost him in the yard. He has beautiful feathers and a long beak.

Unit 04 **A Fun School Festival** pp. 118~119

Step 2

B 1. on → The science festival will start on Thursday at 2:00 p.m.

2. on, at → The talent show will start on Friday at 3:00 p.m.

3. Please visit → Please visit the science classroom.

4. visit the auditorium → Please visit the auditorium.

5. There will be → There will be a poster presentation.

6. will be many → There will be many performances.

Step 3

A 1. The sports event will start on Saturday at 10:00 a.m. 스포츠 행사가 토요일 오전 10시에 시작할 거예요.

2. Please visit the gym. 체육관을 방문해 보세요.

3. There will be a running race. 달리기 경주가 있을 거예요.

4. The cooking show will start on Wednesday at 11:00 a.m. 요리 쇼가 수요일 오전 11시에 시작할 거예요.

5. Please visit the cooking room. 요리실을 방문해 보세요.

6. There will be a cooking competition after.
   이후에 요리 경연 대회가 있을 거예요.

B The art exhibition will start on Sunday at 11:00 a.m. Please visit the art room. There will be exhibits of students' drawings.

07 Review Test pp. 120~121

A 1. park, black

2. visit, concert

3. Tuesday, stadium

B 1. We can have fun together.

2. I can fish in the river.

3. I am looking for my dog.

4. She has black fur.

5. The school festival will start on Wednesday at 3:00 p.m.

C 1. Let's go to the beach.

2. The dress is really awesome.

3. You are so friendly.

4. I lost her at the bus stop.

5. Please visit the auditorium.

6. There will be a running race.

D 1. The art exhibition will **start** on Sunday at 11:00 a.m.

2. **I am** looking for my parrot.

3. **It has** beautiful feathers and a long beak.

4. Thank you for the **sunglasses**.

5. What **are** you doing this Monday?

6. We can see pandas.

Unit 05 Last Vacation
pp. 123~124

Step 2

B 1. did you do → What did you do last spring vacation?

2. last summer → What did you do last summer vacation?

3. I went fishing → I went fishing on a lake.

4. at the beach → I went surfing at the beach.

5. I visited → I visited my grandparents, too.

6. joined a robot → I joined a robot class, too.

Step 3

A 1. What did you do last winter vacation?
지난 겨울 방학에 뭐 했어?

2. I went bowling with my friends.
나는 친구들과 볼링을 치러 갔어.

3. I visited my uncle, too. 나는 삼촌도 방문했어.

4. What did you do last spring vacation?
지난 봄 방학에 뭐 했어?

5. I went camping with my family.
나는 가족이랑 캠핑을 갔어.

6. I learned to dance, too. 나는 춤추는 것도 배웠어.

B A: What did you do last summer vacation?

B: I went kayaking in the river. I joined a science camp, too.

Unit 06 Finding Lost Items
pp. 126~127

Step 2

B 1. I found this → I found this in the playground.

2. found this in → I found this in the music room.

3. Whose cell phone is → Whose cell phone is it?

4. Whose bag is it → Whose bag is it?

5. I think that → I think that it's Olivia's.

6. think, it's Emily's → I think that it's Emily's.

Step 3

A 1. I found these in the gym.
나 이것들을 체육관에서 발견했어.

2. Whose shoes are they? 이거 누구 신발이야?

3. I think that they are Amella's. 그거 아멜라 거 같아.

4. I found this in the art room. 나 이거 미술실에서 발견했어.

5. Whose bottle is it? 이거 누구 병이야?

6. I think that it's Milo's. 그거 마일로 거 같아.

B A: I found this in the science lab. Whose notebook is it?

B: I think that it's Dave's.

Unit 07 My Dream Job
pp. 129~130

Step 2

B 1. I want to → I want to be a soccer player.

2. to be a chef → I want to be a chef.

3. I like to → I like to play soccer.

4. to cook new food → I like to cook new food.

5. Playing soccer → Playing soccer is like an adventure.

6. Cooking is like → Cooking is like magic.

Step 3

A 1. I want to be a dancer. 나는 댄서가 되고 싶어요.

2. I like to dance. 나는 춤추는 것을 좋아해요.

3. Dancing is like a movie. 춤추는 것은 영화 같아요.

4. I want to be a singer. 나는 가수가 되고 싶어요.

5. I like to sing songs. 나는 노래 부르는 것을 좋아해요.

6. Singing is like a story. 노래하는 것은 이야기와 같아요.

B I want to be a police officer. I like to help people. Helping people is like being a hero.

Unit 08 Gift Ideas
pp. 132~133

Step 2

B 1. I want → I want a skateboard for my birthday gift.

2. clay for my → I want clay for my Children's Day gift.

3. I can ride → I can ride it in the park.

4. get rid of → I can get rid of stress.

5. A skateboard is → A skateboard is fast.

6. Clay is soft → Clay is soft.

A 1. I want chocolate for my Christmas gift.
나는 크리스마스 선물로 초콜릿을 받고 싶어요.

2. I can feel happy. 나는 행복함을 느낄 수 있어요.

3. Chocolate is delicious. 초콜릿은 맛있어요.

4. I want new shoes for my New Year's Day gift.
나는 새해 선물로 새 신발을 받고 싶어요.

5. I can run faster. 나는 더 빨리 달릴 수 있어요.

6. New shoes are necessary. 새 신발이 필요해요.

B I want a cookbook for my Christmas gift. I can cook anything with it. A cookbook is helpful.

08 Review Test pp. 134~135

A 1. glasses, Emma's
2. cook new food, magic
3. Christmas, fun

B 1. I went skiing on a mountain.
2. I found these glasses in the classroom.
3. I want to be a cartoonist.
4. We can read new books.
5. I learned Chinese, too.

C 1. Whose cell phone is this?
2. I went kayaking in the river.
3. I visited my uncle, too.
4. Playing soccer is like an adventure.
5. I can ride it in the park.
6. A cookbook is helpful.

D 1. I **want** clay **for** my Children's Day gift.
2. Helping people **is** like **being** a hero.
3. A skateboard r **is** fast.
4. I **like** to dance.
5. I **found** this in the science lab.
6. I think that **it's** Dave's.

Going to the Doctor pp. 137~138

B 1. have a headache → I have a headache.
2. I have a toothache → I have a toothache.
3. I didn't → I didn't do my homework today.
4. didn't eat lunch today → I didn't eat lunch today.
5. went to bed → I went to bed early.
6. went to the dentist → I went to the dentist.

A 1. I have a backache. 나는 허리가 아파요.
2. I didn't take P.E. class today.
나는 오늘 체육 수업을 듣지 않았어요.
3. I went to the nurse's office. 나는 보건실에 갔어요.
4. I have a sore throat. 나는 목이 아파요.
5. I didn't say a word today. 나는 오늘 한 마디도 안 했어요.
6. I went to the doctor. 나는 병원에 갔어요.

B I have a rash. I didn't meet my friend today. I talked on the phone with her.

My Day pp. 140~141

B 1. Let me tell → Let me tell you about my afternoon.
2. me tell you → Let me tell you about my evening.
3. I have lunch → I have lunch at 12 o'clock.
4. have dinner at → I have dinner at 7 o'clock.
5. I play with → I play with my friend after school.
6. walk my dog → I walk my dog after dinner.

A 1. Let me tell you about my Sunday.
나의 일요일에 대해 말해 줄게.
2. I get up late at about 9 a.m. 나는 오전 9시쯤 늦게 일어나.
3. I have brunch with my family.
나는 가족들과 브런치를 먹어.
4. Let me tell you about my Saturday.
나의 토요일에 대해 말해 줄게.
5. I jog around the park at 7 o'clock.
나는 7시에 공원 주변을 조깅해.
6. I read a book all day. 나는 온종일 책을 읽어.

B Let me tell you about my Sunday. I watch a movie at about 3 p.m. I eat popcorn and drink cola.

<hr>

Unit 11 **Safety Rules**   pp. 143~144

Step 2

B 1. Here are the museum → Here are the museum rules.
2. are the zoo rules → Here are the zoo rules.
3. Be quiet around → Be quiet around the exhibits.
4. careful near the pond → Be careful near the pond.
5. Don't eat in → Don't eat in the museum.
6. Don't feed the animals → Don't feed the animals.

Step 3

A 1. Here are the bus rules. 여기 버스 규칙들이 있어요.
2. Stay in your seat. 자리에 앉아 계세요.
3. Don't shout. 소리치지 마세요.
4. Here are the library rules. 여기 도서관 규칙들이 있어요.
5. Be quiet, please. 조용히 해 주세요.
6. Don't draw in the books. 책에 그림 그리지 마세요.

B Here are the pool rules. Wear a swimming cap, please. Don't litter at the swimming pool.

<hr>

Unit 12 **Flea Market Advertisements**
pp. 146~147

Step 2

B 1. These boots are → These boots are so cute.
2. jeans are so → These jeans are so fashionable.
3. They are only → They are only five dollars.
4. are only six → They are only six dollars.
5. You can wear → You can wear the boots in winter.
6. can wear → You can wear the jeans to a party.

Step 3

A 1. These shorts are so stylish. 이 반바지는 아주 멋져요.
2. They are only two dollars. 그것은 겨우 2달러예요.
3. You can wear the shorts in summer.
당신은 여름에 그 반바지를 입을 수 있어요.
4. These shoes are so comfortable. 이 신발은 아주 편해요.
5. They are only four dollars. 그것은 겨우 4달러예요.
6. You can walk a lot with them in the playground.
당신은 그것을 신고 운동장에서 많이 걸을 수 있어요.

B These sandals are so trendy. They are only five dollars. You can wear the sandals outside.

<hr>

09 **Review Test**   pp. 148~149

A 1. morning, get up
2. nice, run
3. pretty, wear

B 1. I have a cold.
2. I have dinner at 7 o'clock.
3. Don't eat in the museum.
4. They are only two dollars.
5. I walk my dog after dinner.

C 1. These shorts are so stylish.
2. They are only four dollars.
3. Don't feed the animals.
4. I watch a movie at about 3 p.m.
5. Let me tell you about my Saturday.
6. I have a backache.

D 1. You can wear the sandals outside.
2. Here are the pool rules.
3. Don't draw in the books.
4. Be careful near the pond.
5. I eat popcorn and drink cola.
6. I didn't say a word.

<hr>

PART **4** **순서를 나타내는 글쓰기**

<hr>

Unit 01 **Doing House Chores**   pp. 153~154

Step 2

B 1. First, plug → First, plug the power cord into an outlet.
2. dust the furniture → First, dust the furniture.
3. Second, switch → Second, switch on the power.
4. vacuum the carpet → Second, vacuum the carpet.

5. Last, push → Last, push the vacuum gently.

6. Last, arrange → Last, arrange the cushions neatly.

Step 3

A 1. First, fill the watering can. 먼저, 물뿌리개에 물을 채워요.

2. Second, go to the flower beds.
두 번째로 화단으로 가요.

3. Last, water the flowers. 마지막으로 꽃에 물을 줘요.

4. First, collect the paper, plastic, and glass.
먼저, 종이와 플라스틱, 그리고 유리를 모아요.

5. Second, sort them into bins.
두 번째로 그것들을 쓰레기통에 분류해요.

6. Last, take them to a recycling center.
마지막으로 그것들을 재활용센터로 가져가요.

B First, make a shopping list. Second, go to the store and pick up a shopping basket. Last, place the groceries in the shopping basket.

Unit 02 **Finding the Way**   pp. 156~157

Step 2

B 1. First, take → First, take the subway.

2. walk straight → First, walk straight.

3. Next, get → Next, get off at Central Station.

4. cross the road → Next, cross the road.

5. Last, turn → Last, turn left at the corner.

6. Last, turn right → Last, turn right at the corner.

Step 3

A 1. First, walk straight. 먼저, 쭉 앞으로 걸어가세요.

2. Next, go straight two blocks.
그 다음에 두 블록을 곧장 가세요.

3. Last, turn right at the corner.
마지막으로 코너에서 오른쪽으로 도세요.

4. First, take the bus. 먼저, 버스를 타세요.

5. Next, get off at the mall. 그 다음에 쇼핑몰에서 내리세요.

6. Last, go down the street. 마지막으로 길을 따라 가세요.

B First, walk to the end of the road. Next, turn right at the corner. Last, cross the road.

Unit 03 **Talking About the Past**   pp. 159~160

Step 2

B 1. One day, went → One day, I went to the zoo.

2. I went to → One day, I went to a city.

3. Then, I saw → Then, I saw some animals there.

4. saw some, there → Then, I saw some buildings there.

5. Later, I took → Later, I took pictures of penguins.

6. took pictures → Later, I took pictures of skyscrapers.

Step 3

A 1. One day, I went to the country. 어느 날, 나는 시골에 갔어요.

2. Then, I saw some farm animals there.
그리고, 나는 거기에서 농장 동물들을 봤어요.

3. Later, I took pictures of cows.
나중에 나는 소들 사진을 찍었어요.

4. One day, I went to the sea. 어느 날, 나는 바다에 갔어요.

5. Then, I saw some sea animals there.
그리고, 나는 거기에서 바다 동물들을 봤어요.

6. Later, I took pictures of dolphins.
나중에 나는 돌고래들 사진을 찍었어요.

B One day, I went to a mountain. Then, I saw some trees there. Later, I took pictures of pine trees.

Unit 04 **Talking About Fairy Tales**   pp. 162~163

Step 2

B 1. Once → Once upon a time, there lived a girl named Cinderella.

2. there lived → Once upon a time, there lived a girl named Alice.

3. One day → One day, she wanted to go to a ball.

4. she fell into → One day, she fell into a hole.

5. In the end → In the end, the fairy godmother helped her.

6. it was all → In the end, it was all a dream.

Step 3

A 1. Once upon a time, there lived three little pigs.
옛날 옛적에 아기 돼지 삼 형제가 살았어요.

2. One day, they built their own houses.
어느 날, 그들은 각자 자기 집을 지었어요.

3. In the end, the third pig's house was the best of them. 결국 셋째 돼지의 집이 그것들 중 최고였어요.

4. Once upon a time, there lived a boy named Jack.
옛날 옛적에 잭이라는 한 소년이 살았어요.

5. One day, he climbed a beanstalk.
어느 날, 그는 콩나무 줄기를 기어올라 갔어요.

6. In the end, he became rich. 마침내 그는 부자가 됐어요.

B Once upon a time, there lived a girl named Goldilocks. One day, she entered the Three Bears' house. In the end, they came home, and she ran away.

10 Review Test

pp. 164~165

A
1. garden, insects
2. Once, there
3. put, make

B
1. Plug the power cord into an outlet.
2. I take the subway.
3. I went to a city.
4. Once upon a time, there lived a girl named Alice.
5. She fell into a hole.

C
1. Second, switch on the power.
2. Last, go straight to the police station.
3. Then, I saw some buildings there.
4. Later, I took pictures of skyscrapers.
5. One day, they ran a race.
6. First, make a shopping list.

D
1. In the end, **he** became rich.
2. One day, **I** went to a mountain.
3. First, **walk** to the end of the road.
4. Next, **cross** the road.
5. Last, **go** grocery shopping.
6. Once upon a time, there lived a girl named Cinderella.

Unit 05 Getting Ready for Outdoor Activities

pp. 167~168

Step 2

B
1. First, I put on → First, I put on a coat and a hat.
2. I put on sunglasses → First, I put on sunglasses.
3. Next, I get → Next, I get gloves.
4. I get a tube → Next, I get a tube.
5. Then, I go → Then, I go to the playground.
6. I go to → Then, I go to the sea.

Step 3

A
1. First, I put on hiking boots. 우선, 나는 등산화를 신어요.
2. Next, I get a backpack. 그 다음에, 나는 배낭을 챙겨요.
3. Then, I go to a mountain. 그리고 나서 나는 산에 가요.
4. First, I put on a swimsuit. 우선, 나는 수영복을 입어요.
5. Next, I get swimming goggles.
그 다음에, 나는 물안경을 챙기죠.
6. Then, I go to a swimming pool.
그리고 나서 나는 수영장에 가요.

B First, I put on a sweatsuit. Next, I get a jump rope. Then, I go to a park.

Unit 06 Talking About Future Plans

pp. 170~171

Step 2

B
1. First, I am → First, I am going to a movie theater.
2. I am going to → First, I am going to a café.
3. Then, am going → Then, I am going to buy a ticket and snacks.
4. I am going to → Then, I am going to buy a hot chocolate.
5. Last, am going to → Last, I am going to watch a movie.
6. I am going to → Last, I am going to drink it.

Step 3

A
1. First, I am going to a bookstore.
우선, 나는 서점에 갈 거예요.
2. Then, I am going to buy a book.
그리고 나서, 나는 책을 살 거예요.
3. Last, I am going to read it. 마지막으로 그것을 읽을 거예요.

4. First, I am going to a clothing store.
   우선, 나는 옷 가게에 갈 거예요.

5. Then, I am going to buy a T-shirt.
   그러고 나서, 나는 티셔츠를 살 거예요.

6. Last, I am going to wear it. 마지막으로 그것을 입을 거예요.

B First, I am going to a toy store. Then, I am going to buy a toy car. Last, I am going to play with it.

Unit 07   **Making Desserts**   pp. 173~174

Step 2

B 1. First, put ice cream → First, put ice cream in a bowl.
   2. mix flour → First, mix flour and eggs.
   3. Then, add → Then, add whipped cream and cherries.
   4. add sugar → Then, add sugar and butter.
   5. Last, sprinkle → Last, sprinkle peanuts on top. Enjoy!
   6. bake a cake → Last, bake a cake. Enjoy!

Step 3

A 1. First, squeeze some oranges into a glass.
      먼저, 유리잔에 오렌지 몇 개를 짜세요.
   2. Then, add sugar to it.
      그러고 나서, 그것에 설탕을 추가하세요.
   3. Last, stir it well. 마지막으로 그것을 잘 저으세요.
   4. First, pour milk and ice cream into a cup.
      먼저, 컵에 우유와 아이스크림을 부으세요.
   5. Then, blend the ingredients.
      그러고 나서, 그 재료들을 섞으세요.
   6. Last, top with whipped cream and some chocolate.
      마지막으로 휘핑 크림과 초콜릿으로 장식하세요.

B First, pour some cereal into a bowl. Then, add some milk to it. Last, add some toppings and eat it. Enjoy!

Unit 08   **How to Save the Earth**   pp. 176~177

Step 2

B 1. First, I can → First, I can ride a bike.
   2. I can walk → First, I can walk.
   3. Second, I can → Second, I can reuse old furniture.
   4. I can reuse → Second, I can reuse old toys.
   5. Last, I can → Last, I can recycle glass.

6. I can recycle → Last, I can recycle paper.

Step 3

A 1. First, I can ride a bus. 먼저, 나는 버스를 탈 수 있어요.
   2. Second, I can reuse old books.
      두 번째로, 헌 책들 재사용할 수 있죠.
   3. Last, I can recycle cans.
      마지막으로 나는 캔을 재활용할 수 있어요.
   4. First, I can carpool.
      먼저, 나는 카풀을 할 수 있어요.
   5. Second, I can reuse old batteries.
      두 번째로, 오래된 배터리를 재사용할 수 있죠.
   6. Last, I can recycle boxes.
      마지막으로 나는 상자들을 재활용할 수 있어요.

B First, I can turn off the water. Second, I can reuse old bags. Last, I can recycle bottles.

---

11   **Review Test**   pp. 178~179

A 1. movie theater, watch
   2. Cut, mix
   3. furniture, glass

B 1. I put on a raincoat and boots.
   2. I am going to buy flowers.
   3. First, peel fruits.
   4. I can turn off the lights.
   5. I get an umbrella.

C 1. I go to a playground.
   2. I can ride a bike.
   3. Bake a cake.
   4. Put ice cream in a bowl.
   5. I am going to a café.
   6. I put on hiking boots.

D 1. **I** go to a swimming pool.
   2. **I** get a jump rope.
   3. **I am going to a** toy store.
   4. Add some milk to it.
   5. **Pour** some cereal into a bowl.
   6. **I can** recycle bottles.

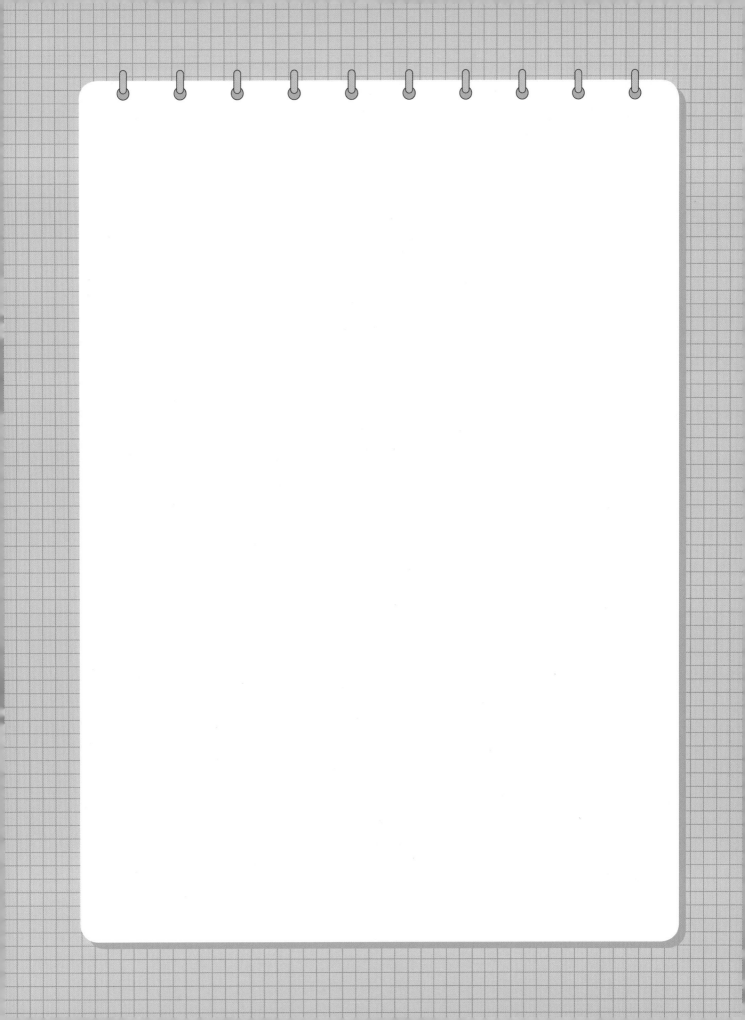